P9-APU-470

JESUS CAN...

GIVE YOU A NEW LIFE!

Christian Writers Collective, LLC
Stephanie K. Reynolds, Founder

Jesus Can... Give You a New Life

Copyright © 2021 by Christian Writers Collective, LLC

Stephanie K. Reynolds, Founder

All rights reserved. No parts of this publication may be reproduced, stored in a retrieval system, or transmitted in any form or by any means—electronic, mechanical, photocopying, recording, scanning or other—except for brief quotations in critical reviews or articles, without the prior written permission of the publisher.

Scripture quotations are from the King James Version unless otherwise noted.

Scriptures marked NIV are taken from *THE HOLY BIBLE: New International Version* ©1978 by the New York International Bible Society, used by permission of Zondervan Bible Publishers.

Scriptures marked NKJV are taken from the New King James Version®. Copyright © 1982 by Thomas Nelson, Inc. Used by permission. All rights reserved.

Book cover design by Virtually Possible Designs

ISBN 978-0-5789-3595-9 (paperback)

ISBN 978-0-5789-3597-3 (ebook)

Dedication

This book is dedicated to my mom, Marion Reynolds, who became my sister-in-Christ on February 23, 2014, and then joined Jesus in Heaven, 3 months later. It's also dedicated to my best friend, Mrs. Naomi Walker, who then became a much-needed spiritual mother to me. When she went to Heaven on my 61st birthday, Oct 8, 2019, she breathed new life into my determination to finally get the *Jesus Can...* series into print. May there be many more books published as part of this series and may many, many, more people discover the truth about Heaven as a result of reading these books.

Table of Contents

Introduction

*This introduction is a continuation
of the dedication in greater detail.*

I have no regrets about helping my dad to care for his bride of 58 years for the last 9 months of her life on this earth. However, the months spent living at my parents' house, instead of having a paying job, left my finances and my work history in a mess. Mom's hospice nurse had often complimented me on the excellence and dignity of the care I provided to Mom. She suggested that I consider becoming a professional caregiver. This seemed like a great idea because it made what was once a gap in my employment history, valuable experience.

At first, it felt like a blessing from the Lord when I landed a job in my new profession less than a week after Mom had passed. But, at the Orientation Meeting, when the owner of the agency asked each of his new employees to share why they had become a caregiver, I burst into tears when it was my turn to answer. This was my first clue that I may have gone back to work too soon. This was confirmed when I quit my job as a caregiver exactly one year later because I was suffering from a severe case of "caregiver burnout." This time, to avoid having a gap in my work history, I had applied for and was hired for a seasonal job before I quit.

Through all the job and other changes in my life since Mom went to Heaven, my friendship with Mrs. Naomi Walker was a comforting constant. We met at the second church I had ever attended. I stayed at the church where I'd gotten saved and went through the ugliest parts of an ugly divorce for 5 years. My son, whom I was expecting when I'd gotten saved there, was 4 1/2 years old when I changed churches for the first time.

I believe that it was providence, not coincidence, that Mom and Mrs. Walker were the same age. I don't remember exactly how it went, but I imagine that Mrs. Walker smiled and embraced my son and I, together, with that same warm and welcoming cheerfulness that we had only experienced from my Mom, up until that point. The bond was instant. She became a friend, a Spiritual Mom to me and a second Grandma to my son, who had never met his dad's mother. [NOTE: This is part of the gaslighting process you'll read about in my testimony: the perpetrator will make sure that his victim never meets anyone who can and/or might tell them the truth about him. Ladies, gentlemen too, for that matter, please take my advice: don't even think about getting serious with someone before you've been to their home and met their parent(s), siblings, and other family and friends. When you say, "I do," you will marry all of these people, for better or worse, not just your spouse! I'm tempted to say, "I wish my parents had told me this before I got married." But my marrying stupidly was not my parents' fault. Now that I've graduated from the School of Hard Knocks, I can admit to you and to myself, "I wish I would have listened and obeyed when my parents tried to warn me!" But I digress...]

As I said, Mrs. Walker was a constant through over three decades of changes in my life. From 29 to 60, I changed jobs and/or businesses more times than I care to admit. Every long and short-term friendship I had ended during those 30 years. Mrs. Walker was my only friend when I decided to go back to college online in 2016. At the age of 57, I finally enrolled to pursue the bachelor's degree I had failed to complete in order to rebelliously elope with my future ex-husband. Consequently, she became the only person who knew how the Lord was giving me step-by-step instructions for founding the Christian Writers Cooperative. (This was the name of my God-given dream business until I was required to change it in August 2020 in order to incorporate.)

Rather than repeat some of the details that you'll read in my testimony, I'll jump to the fact that Mrs. Walker was diagnosed with cancer that took her life on earth and gave her a new life in Heaven with Jesus on October 8, 2019, my 61st birthday. My relentless drive to finally launch the *Jesus Can...* book series was born on that day.

Thank you, Jesus; Mom and Dad; my son, Steven; Mrs. Walker; and the long list of my brothers and sisters in Christ who helped make this book possible, starting with our first 30 CWC members/writers, our editor, our marketing team and our publisher.

I also want to thank you, for picking up a copy of this book. May it help you to believe and spread the word that Jesus CAN DO ANYTHING!

1

Good Friends and the Good News

▼

by Stephanie Reynolds
Founder of the Christian
Writers Collective, LLC

Moving from the "hood" to the suburbs of Milwaukee in 1969, when I was 10, changed my life. I quickly learned that nice and not-so-nice people came in all colors, especially at school. There, the white kids laughed at my ebonic accent. When bussing brought more than four other black kids to the suburbs, they called me an "Uncle Tom" for sounding white!

Even so, I managed to make several good friends at school. Two of them loved me enough to tell me about Jesus, the first when I was 14, and the second when she visited me in Tucson when I was 21 and pursuing a BS in Architecture from the University of Arizona. Each time, I thought my friend was crazy, but I was perfectly "normal."

Right after my crazy friend returned to Milwaukee, a man I'd dated for just two months before leaving for college, moved to nearby Phoenix. Homesickness contributed to mixed emotions about this. I was looking forward to going to college "unattached" for 1,200 reasons. That's how much the round-trip flight to my first boyfriend's military base had cost me. He dumped me shortly after my arrival.

It took me over 30 years to realize why I wisely chose to not reconcile with my first boyfriend after he apologized, but I stupidly chose to accept everything my future ex-husband told me, even when I knew he was lying. It was pride.

Pride made me an easy target for gaslighting, a psychological manipulation tactic. From the moment he arrived in Phoenix, until I filed for divorce in Milwaukee, almost five years later, pride led me to believe and do things I should not have when it came to this man. It was my pride, not my ex, that had cost me everything, starting with my college savings and my self-respect. Thankfully, I wound up pregnant four months after we rebelliously eloped. The despair created by being married to an unfaithful man drove me to consider suicide, but, my innocent, unborn child gave me a reason to live.

Remember my friend from Milwaukee who came to see me in Tucson? When she told me again about Jesus being able to give me a new life, she didn't sound crazy anymore! A new life was exactly what I needed and wanted.

On Sunday, April 10, 1983, while I was at church with my future ex-husband, which was a miracle in itself considering I didn't "do church" and he hadn't attended for years, I received my new life. God knew exactly what it would take for me to lay aside my pride and start living the life He had planned for me rather than the lie I was living to save face. A few weeks later, He used my Christian friend and her husband to transport me and my 11 month old son back where we needed to be at my parents' house.

My son is now 37 years old. He became my brother in Christ

when he was 4 1/2. The highest compliment I could pay my son is to say that even if he wasn't my son, I'd admire the character of the godly man he has become. Founding the Christian Writers Collective is the first fruit of my desire to reach the high bar he has set. But in my role as a godly parent, I also want to be obedient to Proverbs 13:22, which says we're to "leave an inheritance for our children's children."

My best friend, Mrs. Naomi Walker, was the only person I told that Jesus was prompting me to return to college at age 57 because of Proverbs 13:22. I had planned to complete a BS in Business & Communications. She was also the only one who knew how He was rewarding my obedience with step-by-step instructions for founding the CWC. Every essay and term paper I wrote paved a clearer path to success! For the next four years, she enthusiastically and professionally proofread everything I wrote from college papers to resumes. Words alone can't express what an encouragement she was to me.

When Mrs. Walker died on my 61st birthday, October 8, 2019, I knew it was God's providence, not coincidence. She had demonstrated her belief in me and the CWC with her friendship, her enthusiasm, and her tireless proofreading. I pray the Lord would allow me to honor her by dedicating our first book to her, Jesus Can... Give You A New Life! Amen.

UPDATE: July 2021 – I'll let you in on a little CWC insider secret . . . this UPDATE is an UPDATE of an UPDATE! My Editor, Nyla Kay Wilkerson (author of Chapter 19), and I became good friends as we worked tirelessly to complete our original editing deadline of December 15, 2020. We didn't make it.

The list of business, personal, and financial issues that have delayed the printing of this first book of the Jesus Can book series have been many. Some of those reasons are still painful to recall. But the enemy's intense opposition to these books serves to confirm God's intent to use them mightily.

I'm so grateful to all 29 of the other authors who, by faith, submitted their testimony to a start-up business/ministry that could only offer them a byline, extra work, and potential earnings "one of these days." I thank you all for joining me in walking by faith, not by sight. (2 Cor 5:7)

There are so many more people who I would like to thank and will probably take the time to do so in the next book of our series, *Jesus Can... Heal Your Hurts*, which we also hope to release in 2021. But for now, I just want to thank the two greatest gifts God has ever given me in addition to my salvation in Jesus Christ: my dad, Willie C. Reynolds and my son,

Steven W. Reynolds. To say that I couldn't have done this without the both of you is a huge understatement. I thank you both for putting up with this dreamer for 62 years and 37 years, respectively. May the Lord richly reward your love, patience, tolerance, and support with His greatest gifts. Amen.

Stephanie Reynolds, CWC Founder

2

From Feminism to Faith

▼

by Kitty Foth-Regner

Sometime between May 2000 and August 2001, I went from being a lifelong feminist, atheist, science writer to becoming a born-again follower of Jesus Christ.

The catalyst to my spiritual journey was the death of my beloved Christian mother. I had to know if this God of hers might really exist and might actually have called her to some heavenly home. If so, I had to figure out how to get there myself. If there was an eternity to be spent anywhere, I didn't want to spend it apart from her.

Is there a God?

That was my starting point. Much to my surprise, it was an easy question to answer.

That was largely because of the writings of the Intelligent Design movement, represented by an organization of many Ph.D. scientists. They have amassed overwhelming evidence proving there's an intelligent designer, without saying exactly who that might be.

In this phase, I was stunned to learn that there are really only two options: the universe came into existence via this intelligent designer or through random chance over vast ages.

Of all the evidence they presented to demonstrate the truth of the former, a list of what I found most impressive would start with:

- The anthropic principle, which says that all the allegedly random values in the universe's physics are precisely the values needed to support life.

- The fact of irreducible complexity, which underscores the countless biological systems that are too complex and mutually dependent to have been formed through the tiny, independent modifications that are essential to evolution.

- The lack of any mechanism through which evolution could unfold— "natural selection" being simply Quality Control, and mutations being exclusively neutral or negative.

After just a month of study, I could see that there must have been a creator—in short, a God.

Which God is the real deal?

Early on, I learned that there are essentially only two kinds of worldview that admit to a God:

- Christianity, which says that the ticket into the afterlife is repenting of our sins and trusting in Jesus Christ to have paid their penalty on the cross.

- Everything else, from Islam to Hinduism to the New Age, which all say that the ticket into the afterlife is being a good person.

I began my search for the real God by investigating Everything else. My reasoning: my mom had been a good person, I could become one, and that way I could avoid all the boring Christian stuff I had been raised on. Trouble is, I spent months digging deeply for evidence that one of these religions was true—and came up empty. "Because we have a holy book" is not proof, nor is "Because there are so many of us" or "Because it works."

Finally, I threw up my hands and picked up the Bible—and was blown away by what I found. The main reason: literally dozens of scientific facts that its ancient writers could not possibly have known apart from divine inspiration—facts from the sun having its own orbit (proven by modern science in about 1999) to the earth being round (mentioned by the biblical prophet Isaiah two centuries before Pythagoras, who normally gets the credit). This was the stuff of epiphany. It took me 90% of the way to certainty that the Bible is true, and that it tells us what we need to know about both God and man's past, present, and future.

There was much more, including the Bible's uncanny prophetic accuracy. As a college history minor who had focused on the modern 20th century, I was most immediately impressed by the Bible's detailed predictions about the restoration of the nation of Israel. It happened in May 1948, just as the Bible had said it would in its books written 2000 to 3000 years ago.

Then, there were the scores of Old Testament predictions about the Messiah Himself. It turns out that Jesus fulfilled every last one, most involving events beyond His control. Could these ancient prophets have made such precise predictions without the help of a supernatural being who exists outside of time?

I could not see how.

In the end, I was convinced: There is a God. He is the God of the Bible. If we have any concern about our eternities, we'd best pay attention to the only book He has ever inspired.

Kitty Foth-Regner

Kitty Foth-Regner spent her 40 year copywriting career specializing in scientific subjects. So, it is no surprise that it was the Bible's scientific truth that led her to Christ—a journey she recounted in her memoir Heaven Without Her. A long-term-care volunteer since 2000, she's also published The Song of Sadie Sparrow, a novel exploring the relationships of three women whose paths cross in an idyllic nursing home.

Visit her at www.EverlastingPlace.com.

3

I Cried When God Called Me

▼

by Charles E. Jackson II

Every time the doors of the church were open—no matter the day, time, or type of service—I was there. Such is the life of a PK, or preacher's kid, right? Growing up in a home with a devout Christian mother and church elder, there was no asking questions, playing sick, or putting any other activity in place of attending church. Although I lived under very sound Biblical teachings and participated in various church functions, the moment my mom stopped dragging me to church, I stopped going.

Once I left home, I lived for myself. I may have prayed before a meal or for divine help on an exam I didn't study for, but other than that, I had no desire to serve God the way I saw my mother serve Him all my life. I had a very nice bachelor pad, a brand-new car, and enjoyed the finer things in life because of my income as a commissioned salesman. Life was great! Then one day, I attended a church service, and everything changed. As I sat in the back of the church during worship, suddenly, I felt a wave of emotions overtake me. My heart became heavy. I had an overwhelming feeling that my life was empty.

I needed God, so I stood up and walked toward the altar. I was out of order and didn't know what I was going to do. I was drawn to the altar like a moth to a flame, and I wasn't stopping! Walking past the worship leader, I knelt at the altar and began to cry out to God for salvation. I remember asking Jesus to forgive me of my sins, come into my heart, and be Lord over my life. After what seemed like a few minutes, but I later learned was quite some time, I stood.

Everyone in the church was on their feet, either crying, praying, or staring in awe of whatever had just taken place. I felt as light as a feather and as free as a bird. The pastor gave me the mic and asked if I wanted to say anything. I took it and began to speak what was on my heart. Before I was done, there were about seven or eight other people kneeling at the altar, crying out for salvation.

My pastor said there was a calling on my life. He started giving me opportunities to serve and speak to the youth. It all happened so fast. I didn't know what he meant by "called." Nevertheless, I did what I was told. Soon after, I began to run into financial troubles, lost my home, my car, my job, and experienced all types of trials and temptations. I wasn't experiencing the blessings and favor of God that I'd heard other saints testify about all my life. I thought maybe I was to blame. After all, I was leading the Youth Ministry at the bidding of my Pastor.

One day, in the midst of a very difficult trial, I got in my car. While I was driving, I cried and blamed God for my heartache. I remember asking God, "Why are all these things happening to me?" Then, all of a sudden, a scripture, 2 Timothy 4:17, just dropped into my mind. I knew a lot of verses, but I had no clue what scripture this was or why it popped in my head. Quickly, I pulled over and grabbed my Bible.

> *...but the Lord stood at my side, and gave me strength, so that through me, the message of the Gospel might be fully preached, and all the gentiles might hear it. And I was delivered out of the mouth of the lion.* 2 Timothy 4:17

I'd never heard this verse, but immediately I knew two things. First, God had called me to ministry, not my Pastor, and second, everything I was going through was preparing me to boldly proclaim the gospel. Yes, I was going to be used in my ministry calling! In other words, God was giving me the opportunity to see and come to know Him for myself. He was my Savior, provider, protector, healer, deliverer, Lord, king, and righteous judge. From that moment on, I have traveled all over, preaching the gospel. My specific calling is to encourage those suffering while in the process of discovering and starting to walk in their own calling. I'm in the process of writing a devotional on the subject of biblical suffering, that I hope to share with Christians everywhere, one day soon.

Charles E. Jackson II

Charles E. Jackson II is a dynamic speaker, relational leader, and audacious man. Founder of the Relational Leadership Network, an innovative platform connecting leaders and communities worldwide, he is a visionary who understands the power of connection.

4

A Life Changing Ultimatum

▼

by Alan Taylor

I am so thankful to God that He interrupted this self-centered young man many years ago by revealing Himself and changing my life forever. Well, to put that more accurately, He didn't actually change my life, but He replaced the imitation one I thought I had with the real life that He intended for me from before the world began.

I grew up in a stable home with Dad and Mom, four kids, grandparents not too far away, bicycles, plenty of lawn to play on, a cat, and even sheep across the fence. Oh yes, church on

Sunday, Sunday School as a child, and later Youth Group for teenagers, were all part of my life. I only went to Youth Group because I attended an all-boys secondary school. Youth Group was where I was able to mix with the girls.

It was as an adult that I found out I wasn't allowed to go to kindergarten (age 4) on the same day as my friend. Apparently, we would cause too much trouble. Then when I started school (age 5), the class had to walk in two lines, boys on one side and girls on the other, holding hands between the lines. I took one look at the girl opposite me and thought "There's no way I'm holding your hand," so instead, I bit her hand.

Again, my mom waited until I was an adult to tell me that the couple of occasions when she went to a women's rest facility for a week were because of me. It seemed she just needed a break from this boisterous young lad who had a knack for winding her and my sisters up the wrong way. It's not like I had a police record or anything like that, but I definitely had some anti-social and selfish tendencies.

I was in my early twenties when, unknown to me, God had an appointment with me. I had left my hometown following university and was working as a junior accountant. A young lady caught my eye, and we started dating. She was a Christian, but I was okay with that. I was familiar with Christianity from my upbringing. One Sunday night after an evening out, she said with all seriousness, "Alan, I can't go out with you anymore unless you become a Christian." The conviction from those words hit me deep in my soul. Suddenly, everything I had heard growing up confronted me with truth, and I had nowhere to hide. I knew I was going to hell; I knew I needed to turn my life over to Jesus, and I knew I was facing a turning point of my own choosing. I walked, somewhat shattered, back to my apartment, got down on my knees, and turned my life over to Jesus Christ. I knew He was the Savior of the world, but now it was real and personal.

Two nights later my girlfriend had her regular home group meeting, and I went with her. There was no home meeting that evening, instead they were doing some baptisms in the sea. I said, "Well, you'd better baptize me, too, since I received Jesus on Sunday night!" I was joyfully immersed in the surf. A couple of months later the home group leader confessed to me that he had some misgivings about baptizing me. He thought I was faking it for my girlfriend.

Soon after that, the young lady and I broke up, but I was already committed to church, home group, witnessing to my friends, and doing all I could to grow in God. Eighteen months later, I met a wonderful godly woman. We were engaged within three months, and married three months after that.

We committed our marriage to God and said, "God, You take us anywhere, and we'll serve You in whatever capacity You choose."

We have raised a family, undertaken various pastoral roles, as well as had accounting jobs, and experienced surplus and loss. We've seen God's faithfulness over the years during all of these times. The circumstances of life don't change the fact that God is good, and Jesus is the Savior. By God's grace, our three sons have wonderful Christian wives, and we are blessed by an expanding number of grandchildren. Despite these tumultuous times in which we live today, we have an expectancy and excitement about what God is doing and feel we have been prepared to serve Him in these current days.

Alan Taylor

Alan Taylor is a minister of the Word and the Spirit. He lives in the coastal city of Tauranga, New Zealand, with his wife, Lynne. Their passion is to equip the saints to follow their God-given destiny, so they love to inform, impart, and encourage. To maintain balance, Alan loves to run, cycle, and spend time with his family.

5

God Led Me to Freedom When I Gave Him the Reins

▼

by Lloyd Portman

I was born the first child of four in a family that lived in a country town in New Zealand. Soon after I was born my mother suffered a very debilitating bout of postpartum depression and was committed to a mental hospital.

She was so ill they restrained her in a strait jacket for her own protection. She also received shock treatments during the eight months she was restrained in that jacket, and slowly she returned to a manageable state. Finally, after eighteen months away, my mother was able to come home.

During my mother's absence, I was cared for by my father's parents. When Mum returned home, we started living as a family for the first time. As if that beginning wasn't enough stress on the family, sadly there was more to come.

Soon after Mum's return, my father developed bowel cancer and subsequently died on his 26th birthday. From this double hit of abandonment, I became very susceptible to rejection and insecurity.

For me, school was a problem because I had an undiagnosed learning disability—dyslexia. I always struggled with spelling, grammar, and reading to the point where I learned to become an auditory learner, someone who learns through listening. This also led me to become a practical and hands-on person.

Fast forward 26 years...while I was farming and milking cows 365 days of the year, I had an encounter with God and was blessed to be born again. I was so strongly converted that my life was turned upside down.

All I wanted to do was go to Bible College. I felt certain that I was called to the ministry.

God said NO to me about going to Bible College. Instead, the cowshed became my classroom. He met me there every milking time, and this was where He taught me. These were very exciting times! On one occasion, He made a statement to me that I have never forgotten. He said, "Now you have the choice to either walk with Me or with the Church." Because I was very young in my faith, I asked Him what that meant for me. He said, "If you walk with the Church, you will have trouble with Me, and if you walk with Me, you will have trouble with the Church!" Unfortunately, because of my need to be accepted, I decided to do both! I regretted this compromise for the next 20 years.

We subsequently moved to another district, bought a farm, and joined a local congregation. After three years there, God called me to pioneer a church in a neighboring village. This church owned the town's Christian bookstore, which was staffed by five faithful volunteers. I was visiting the bookstore early one morning to select different gifts for each of the staff since it was Christmastime. I had selected some gifts and was about to put them on our account when God spoke to me. He said, "Put the gifts back, take the blank cards home, and give each of them something from the Pastor's desk!"

I was excited about this because I needed Him to show me what to write. I wanted it to be His words. At the time, I was ministering prophetically. God gave me a prophetic word for each person.

The amazing thing about this was each prophetic word was fulfilled within the following year! Each prophecy was a positive word and so naturally each person was ecstatic with their Christmas gift. This was the beginning of my journey as a Poet. God, Himself, is the ultimate Poet, and much of His Word is poetic. I continue to be amazed at how the scriptures unfold to me when He is my tutor.

I now write Christian devotional poetry. This devotional poetry has been used as study materials for small groups and my poetry has been read from pulpits. I've been told that its prophetic edge resonates within people's hearts. The many testimonials I have received confirm that God has led me into this.

Lloyd Portman

My passion is to write poetry that engages my audience in a visceral way, where the words I write, being God-inspired, are read and enter the heart of the readers. I live down under in New Zealand and it's fun connecting with my CWC family during our weekly virtual meetings. I can tell them what tomorrow is about because we are a day ahead!

6

From Thief to Giver

▼

by Lindsey Shuler

My father is a pastor. Maybe you think that makes me auto-matically a Christian or at least predisposed to be one. You have a good point. However, every person in the world makes a choice about how they'll live. At 9, I made the choice to be baptized and, at 12, to be a real Christ-follower. Even after being baptized, very little about my life changed.

That's because, back then, I was addicted to stealing. I stole from stores, from people, and from family members. I found it fun to scheme and plan the act of stealing. After "accomplishing the mission," I always felt like hiding or trying to escape the ugly and dark emotions of being afraid, ashamed, trapped, and condemned. Reading through the Bible and from Sunday school lessons, I realized that I was relying on what Dietrich Bonhoeffer had coined "cheap grace" believing that when I stole, I would be able to say "I repent" and Jesus would forgive me. However, I couldn't stop stealing! Since I was never actually repenting, my heart became increasingly calloused as I continued to steal.

One morning, I read "there is no forgiveness for sin when you know it is sin and continue in it" in Hebrews 10:26. It was as if I was seeing it for the first time. I saw 1 Corinthians 6:9-11 this way, too. Here's what I saw with my eyes and my heart that day:

> *Or do you not know that wrongdoers will not inherit the kingdom of God? Do not be deceived: Neither the sexually immoral nor idolaters nor adulterers nor men who have sex with men nor thieves nor the greedy nor drunkards nor slanderers nor swindlers will inherit the kingdom of God. And that is what some of you were. But you were washed, you were sanctified, you were justified in the name of the Lord Jesus Christ and by the Spirit of our God.*
> 1 Corinthians 6:9-11 (NIV)

It didn't happen quickly, but after that day, I was more aware of stealing being sin. I felt bad when I disobeyed God's Word. I was starting to replace "cheap grace" with genuine repentance.

Eventually, the callus covering my heart started to be worn down, just as the list of people, places, and things that I had stolen, started being recounted in my mind. I prayed, "God, I don't want to steal anymore, but I am addicted to it. Help me stop."

I repeated these prayers many days, but I made no changes to back them. I didn't know how. Finally, at church, the pastor talked about stealing and restitution. This was God answering my prayers and showing me how to repent. Tears flowed as that callus fell off my heart, and I repented of all of my sins. This included all of the stealing and all other things that I knew were not pleasing to God.

I finally realized that repenting meant to confess the sin and stop living with it. I went back to every person and every place, told them what I had done, and paid back what I could. Jesus literally changed my heart. I was no longer weighed down by the darkness, fear, guilt, shame, or other negative things! All were replaced with joy, peace, love, and freedom. Beyond that, I found purpose in my life. I was more gracious, ready to forgive, more empathetic, and more compassionate. When college came, I knew that nursing was where God wanted me to fulfill my life's purpose...at least for a season.

Lindsey Shuler

Hello, my name is Lindsey. I am a nurse residing in the United States of America. Pastimes include reading, walking, exploring, being part of ELI church, and spending quality time with family and my fiancé. Christian Writers Collective appealed to me because I love Jesus and know His love for you. There is none like Him and I want to share: It is possible to have a living relationship with Him!

7

Believing in God Is Different Than Knowing God

▼

by Danielle Christopher

I grew up in Tujunga, California, back when it was a sleepy little town in the 1970s.

My life was about, well, daydreaming, animals, and chores. I lived in a very old home that was said to be an old miner's shack. Where we heard that story, I don't know. I certainly never saw any areas that needed mining. Of course, I always believed it was gold mining since we were so poor and had hoped to find some treasure for ourselves.

My mom and dad divorced when I was in first grade. A year later, Dad married my stepmom. My mom was the best at showing me how to love others, my dad, not so much. With him, it was "his way or the highway."

Most of my time was spent with my mom. We raised chickens, bunnies, ducks, and kitties. She definitely taught me to love God's creatures. Her dad also contributed this way. He'd take the bus to our town and walk up to our little mountain in his 80s, just to take me on a nature walk near Mom's house. He was a light, a light of God, although I was not yet familiar with that.

Mom was always kind to me. She was a sacrificial example for my brother and me. She'd sell her antiques or her camera (animal photography was her passion) to buy food or gifts for us. Two favorite gifts or treasures that I still have at age 56 are the books *First Graces* and *God Is Everywhere.* I still get such joy when I read them!

Dad was harder to be around, due to his demeanor. The "my way or the highway" vibe was always prevalent. It was always lurking in the shadows. He was a good worker, as far as I know, but at home, we were there to wait on his needs. My younger brothers, who came along in the middle and late 1970s, got full doses of the wait on Dad routine, stepmom, Linda, too.

One time, in my elementary years, a man from a local church invited me to services. At that time, I felt uncomfortable with him and didn't go. I didn't yet see that I was being pursued by the loving God, Himself.

Later, in 1977, I finally received a pony. Ladybug was her name, and since I'd waited nearly two years for her, we were inseparable. Well, except for bedtime.

Taking Ladybug out into the hills gave me freedom and also new friends that I wouldn't have otherwise known. My world before was the street that I lived on, Inspiration Way.

When I was about 13, I met a new friend named Kathy. She was fun and I loved being around her! I quickly found out that she was a Christian. I liked that, although all I knew about Christianity was a belief in God. I knew I believed in God, but she told me that I didn't know God. One day she was talking with a friend named Anthony about God. He was debating her in the who, what, and where, of the Lord. She told me I wouldn't understand the conversation, so I left. Her statement really bugged me.

In January 1980, a group of men moved into a home on our street. The guys were quietly going about their lives until the last man moved in. Dan was loud in his music, laughter, and discussions. He talked often about the Lord and told me how I needed to be born again. He showed me scriptures and explained things to me. As I got to know Dan, Cary, Bill, John, and those they took in as a sort of halfway house, it was obvious they were just guys who loved the Lord, loved people, and wanted wives of their own.

In April of 1980, as I lay in bed, I asked the Lord into my life. I asked Him to forgive me of my sins, known and unknown. It was scary at first, but I've never regretted knowing Him.

Life hasn't been easy, but I trust Him with all my details, my fears, my questions, and my life. Through the years, I've looked back on times that I now see as the Lord's pursuit of me, and it's exciting!

On a side note, about the man named Cary, we've been married almost 38 years as of this writing, and I love him dearly.

Danielle Christopher

Hi, I'm Danielle. I live in Tucson, Arizona with my hubby, five cats and Tessie the wonder dog. (Wonder, as in I wonder what she's barking at now.) Oh yes, we also live with and care for my husband's dad. Our kids and grandkids live elsewhere, so besides caretaking, I am finally doing more of the hobbies I started to enjoy years ago.

8

Better Than Money

▼

by Ava Y. Cullen

For the Son of man is come to seek and to save that which was lost. Luke 19:10

I loved having my mornings and afternoons free. Obligation-free left more time for me to explore things for just myself. I could do whatever I wanted, when I wanted to do it, where I wanted, and however it suited me. It was a perfect life! I was single and didn't have any children by choice. My job paid well. I was sitting pretty. I had the trifecta of life.

It didn't matter to me if I was alone or with other people. I loved to dance, eat out, and shop. Being on the go was what I loved. I could equally be satisfied alone or with people.

One day, during one of my financially scant days, I found it boring with little or no money. I decided to go window shopping and to buy myself a nice lunch. First, I found an expensive discount furniture outlet store and started browsing to pass some time. I enjoyed my day even when I knew I wasn't going to get to buy anything. As I moseyed around, a rather large ornate desk caught my eye. It was grand in size, a deep mahogany, and expensive. It was more than $6,000. With that information, I knew I couldn't afford it. I examined it thoroughly and then wandered into the first mall I saw. Since I knew that desk wouldn't be mine, I kept moving.

When I was finished window shopping and satisfied, I slowly sauntered past a few more run-of-the-mill mall offerings. That is until I came across a store called "Things Remembered." Many of the items there were for certain milestones in life. Also, it seemed the gift shop's specialty was engraving. They had lovely things, but only one of them seemed to catch my eye. It was a plaque that read, "I asked Jesus . . . How much do you love me? And He stretched out His arms and died." I stopped dead in my tracks. Frozen there in front of that sign, I kept reading it again and again. Finally, I slowly began to walk away as my eyes welled up with tears. Something made me continue to think about that picture. I began to whimper silently as I left the store.

I forgot about lunch and went home to get ready for work. Since I got home a bit early, I decided to rest. I laid across my bed and fell asleep. It was a few hours later when I awoke. There was plenty of time for me to make it to work. I didn't exactly know why I was in a funk, but I kept to myself all that evening. It was an odd shift. I started at 8:00 PM and ended at 4:30 AM. After work I decided to take a different route home. I was just driving and driving. Finally, I exited the freeway, after realizing and asking myself, "Why am I on the highway?" I exited and continued to drive on the street. My car suddenly stopped at a red light. Looking up I saw a big sign that read: Lighthouse Gospel Chapel. Alone in the car, I heard a soft inaudible voice telling me to go there. I grimaced in confusion. The light turned green. I drove home contemplating what had just happened.

The following Sunday I found myself in that church. I have come to know Jesus in the divine exchange—His righteousness for my sins. He freely gives us salvation from our sins.

Jesus Can...

Repent ye therefore, and be converted, that your sins may be blotted out, when the times of refreshing shall come from the presence of the Lord. Acts 3:19

Ava Y. Cullen

I am a retired teacher, with degrees in Educational Leadership. During my 65 years, I've had various jobs and interests, including working as a beautician, clerk, traveling, teaching Children's Church, and creative arts. As a stroke survivor, I have the opportunity to connect with several personal care workers, daily. I also enjoy spending time with family and friends, watching television, playing Scrabble, writing, Bible Study, and attending Church through ZOOM.

9

I Walked Away from the Self-Righteous Party

▼

by Michelle Jackson

Democrats, Republicans, we've all heard a lot about these parties lately. I am the founder of the Self-Righteous Party. Someone had to die for me to be able to walk away from the party I created, but before I did, I secretly walked to the beat of my own drum while outwardly singing the praises of God.

I built my party's platform upon the things I felt I was doing right in my life. I was a church member and regular attendee, so church attendance was one of my party's most important policies. I had been baptized at five years old, so being baptized was an important part of my party's platform, too. Of course, being a good person had to be part of the Self-Righteous Party platform because—I was. Compared to my twin brother, who had been in and out of jail since youth, I was a very good person. I'd never been to jail.

All was good within my Self-Righteous Party, so all was under control. That is until one evening in July 2008. It was while looking into the window of my lying, cheating husband's car, I saw my true condition. As I held the brick up to smash his window, I noticed my reflection. I didn't look righteous at all. In fact, I looked as far away from righteous as one can get because I looked crazed. Once I closely examined that woman, I never wanted to see her again. I dropped the brick and walked away.

After clearly seeing myself as I truly was, I knew I needed to change. Previously, I had heard only propaganda about God, but now I decided to search for the truth myself. I found exactly what I was seeking.

Relationship

Growing up within a strict religious household, I thought God ran His house the same way. I was just to do as I was told and follow the rules. If not, I could not stay. I either did this or I was going to go to hell. God was just this faraway figure giving rules for life.

I understood Jesus had died because He wanted us to live with Him, but I didn't realize He wanted a relationship, too. The more I read, the more I realized that He wasn't about rules but about relationships. He was only showing me how to maintain an intimate relationship with Him.

Love and Acceptance

I thought that I knew something about love, but I really knew nothing. God loves the little children and God loves me. I'd heard it before in songs, but it was like a foreign language to me, because I didn't understand. Like many girls, I had learned something about love in the romance books I read and was attracted to it. I even saw love in real life sometimes with a dad or mom and their kids, but I had never received it. Love was a stranger. My mom was raised without hugs and without hearing "I love you," so she didn't show that to us kids. My dad left when I was young and had re-married. He was the quiet type, also. I never got any feeling of love from him either. This is why when I heard that Jesus loved me, it didn't mean anything to me.

"He loved me so much that he died for me." This is what I had read in the romance books. The men loved so much that they gladly died. This seemed similar, but His death was much more than this. Jesus loved me before I even knew or loved Him.

Faithfulness

Being around so many unfaithful men, like my ex-husband and father, for example, didn't lead me to have much faith in a Savior and Father I couldn't see. If you couldn't see them, then I thought you couldn't trust them. The only person I felt that I could trust was myself. Even though I adhered to what I was taught for the most part, I did things as I saw fit. I walked to the beat of my own drum, until doing things my way brought me to standing in front of a car with a brick.

Then, I came across His promise that He would never leave me nor forsake me. Not even in death would He leave me, and nothing would separate me from Him. What a great promise! It's like a type of marriage pledge. Unlike man, Jesus wasn't able to lie. Wow did men in my life lie, even for no reason.

The Lord is giving me every reason to trust Him. He's faithful, loving, a great provider, and has the power and authority to cause everything to work out for my good. I accepted His offer. Now I am living my life for Him and He is guiding the steps of my new life.

Therefore, we were buried with Him through baptism into death, that just as Christ was raised from the dead by the glory of the Father, even so we also should walk in newness of life. Romans 6:4 (NKJV)

Michelle Jackson

Michelle Jackson is a Chicago native who has lived in Milwaukee since 2008. By day, she works as an energy-industry analyst. But her lifelong dream is to write fiction and non-fiction exploring, through storytelling, the parallel existence of physical and spiritual laws. Her debut work, *A Prisoner's Pardon,* delves deep into the issue of prison reform as an answer to recidivism, and the Word of God as the truth that can set anyone free.

10

He Made Me for More

▼

by Jill Wright

God's Word tells us, "He shall direct your paths." That is exactly what I experienced. I was in a Bible study, Discerning the Voice of God, in my neighborhood trying, but struggling, to live out that scripture. It is from Proverbs 3:5 and says, "Trust in the Lord with all your heart and lean not on your own understanding; in all your ways acknowledge Him and He shall direct your paths."

I wanted to trust Him, but for some reason, I knew I didn't. The problem was that I wasn't sure why I didn't. I had been feeling burdened, burned out, overwhelmed. My job was demanding and my self-confidence eroding. I was surviving, just barely, one day at a time. It took everything I had to get up in the morning and do life every day.

Most people didn't know how much I was struggling, but my emotional health was at an all-time low. I had prayed for many months for God to show me why I was here and to give me some clue as to my purpose on this earth.

> *For I know the thoughts that I think toward you, says the Lord, thoughts of peace and not of evil, to give you a future and a hope.* Jeremiah 29:11

Our timing is often not God's timing. His timing is perfect. It didn't happen on my timetable, but He began unfolding a new chapter in my life. I prayed for Him to help me trust in Him. I surrendered and He began to work in my life.

First, it was a podcast that a friend recommended. That led me to another podcast about trusting God. Then, another friend was looking for volunteers that she could coach in order to get her life coaching certification.

I looked for a less stressful job, but all the doors I tried to open slammed in my face. God was closing the "wrong" doors so He could open the right ones. It was crystal clear Who was at work. There was no other explanation for the path that was so expertly displayed before me. He would illuminate one step. I would follow Him. Then another step would light up and I would follow.

The more I trusted Him, the easier it was to take that next step, even without knowing how, why, or what the future held. All I knew was that the future held God and that God held me. For the first time in my life, that was enough for me.

There are so many examples of God working in my life. He worked in my husband's heart to pave the way for a series of decisions that my husband would have never agreed to otherwise. From consenting to a huge financial commitment to open my new life coaching business, to leaving my job to do this scary, big new thing, are all evidence of God at work. He orchestrated everything in my circumstances. From working on my boss's heart to allow me to leave earlier than originally agreed, to opening up an earlier spot in the life coaching certification program, I saw that God was working everywhere. What I learned is that I can trust God. When I trust Him, seek Him, listen for His voice, and look for where He is working, I can also trust myself.

Now to Him who is able to do immeasurably more than all we ask or imagine, according to His power that is at work within us, to Him be glory in the church and in Christ Jesus throughout all generations, for ever and ever! Amen. Ephesians 3:20-21

When I trust Him, He always abundantly delivers on His promises. I was praying for a new job, but He wanted to give me a new life. He wanted immeasurably more for me than all I could ask or imagine!

Jill Wright

Jill Wright is a Money Mindset Coach helping equip and empower women to build the life and business they were called to, while leading them to the truth – that they are MADE for MORE. When not working, she enjoys reading, walking or watching turkeys, deer, and other wildlife that frequent her backyard. Jill lives with her husband in Nashville, TN, where they love to help at their church.

11

The Ride Is Better When Jesus Drives

▼

by Kim Patterson

Do you ever look back and wonder, "How did I get here?" The highway of life has so many twists and turns. We mistakenly think we are in the driver's seat.

I grew up in a dysfunctional household. My parents divorced when I was ten and that really began to shape my identity. I believed I was a mistake. I was not wanted by my father and was not enough to hold my family together. There were so many things that were out of my control, but I had found a solution. I'll just work really hard at being perfect. I tried to become the perfect daughter, getting all my chores done, being an "A" student, being protector over my sister, and excelling in sports. I tried very hard not to get into trouble, or at least not get caught. This life had been working for me . . . so far.

When I met my future husband in college, I put my hope in a new family. His family represented television's "The Cunninghams" to me – normal. The image of Norman Rockwell and every fairytale I had come to believe were summed up in this family. I had met my Prince Charming! All I had to do now was to make the shoe fit, move into the castle, click my heels three times, and ride off into the sunset. I falsely believed I was in control of my future. I had to make things happen. Most of the time I used manipulation and over-planning to make things happen. If I could anticipate every obstacle and figure out how to solve it ahead of time, then I would be in control. Again, this life was working for me . . . so far.

It wasn't until after the birth of my second child that I realized that this life of control and perfectionism was exhausting. In fact, it wasn't working as well as I thought. It became more difficult to balance everything. Whoever came up with the term "Supermom" was evil, and yes, I am suggesting it was the enemy tempting women to overwork themselves, spin their wheels, and not see their true identity.

Thankfully, it was about this time that my neighbor suggested we attend their church. I instantly felt at home and found a community of moms with whom I could bond and share life. They were all reading the Bible, so that's what I did. The Word transformed my whole perspective. I didn't realize I was in an identity crisis and performance trap. As I read, I began to see Jesus for the first time. Oh sure, I had attended church before. In fact, I had invited Jesus to come into my heart at the age of eight, but He wasn't "real" to me. He became real the day He helped me find my diamond . . . yes, a real diamond.

One day, I discovered that the stone was no longer in the setting of my diamond ring. I entered into an exhaustive search. After looking everywhere for it, I knew I was going to have to resort to praying. I was going to have to call in the "big guns," those powerful people who seem to have God's ear. Then I thought, "No, I'm going to ask Jesus to help me." I prayed and asked Him to put my diamond somewhere very obvious so I could find it. I suggested the middle of the floor and when I went up to my daughter's nursery, that's exactly where it was. I realized that Jesus is real!

I also realized that I am not in control of everything, Jesus is. I could let go and surrender what I was holding on to so tightly. Jesus was not only holding on to me but holding on to everything in my life. Colossians 1:17 says that "He is before all things, and in Him all things hold together." Ultimately, I was looking for exactly that. No matter how hard I tried, I couldn't hold anything together. Now I knew Someone who could . . . Jesus!

Finally, I am resting in my true identity with the approval of my Heavenly Father. I am experiencing a satisfying homelife and being a godly mother to my now three children. I teach and lead other women concerning how to grow in their faith and how to believe God and all His promises. When I look back on my life, I see a journey in which Jesus has been with me, ever present in the passenger seat. When I let Him in the driver's seat, however, I see that He has taken me . . . so very far.

Kim Patterson

Kim Patterson is a wife and mother of three. She has been a leader in her church for the past 13 years, leading various small groups and teaching Bible studies. Kim has a passion for women's ministries and discipleship. It is her love for the Lord that fuels her desire to see others grow in Christ and walk in freedom and victory.

Kim is the author of *To the Thirsty: Journey Into the Depths of God*. It's available at AbeBooks.com.

12

Blessed Assurance

▼

by Samuel Stewart

I asked Jesus into my heart when I was four, but there is much more to my story. I am a very logical person and have a propensity to overthink things. I have spent a lot of time pondering Jesus. One of the hardest lessons of my life was learning that thinking about Jesus doesn't mean I know Him or that He knows me. That comes much later in my story, but I'm getting ahead of myself.

I grew up in a Christian family and went to a Christian school from kindergarten to eighth grade. One fateful morning at 9:42 AM, the sixth-grade teacher said the morning prayer. I looked up at the clock and saw the class around me with their eyes closed. Was Someone really listening? I logically took my inquiry to the Bible and started reading, but I got discouraged during the detailed account of the tabernacle. The next year, after hearing stories of persecution and martyrdom in other parts of the world, I realized on Easter that Jesus didn't have to die but chose to out of love. During that special church service, I shed a tear, realizing the gravity of that choice. Then, I got serious.

I began an established three-year Bible reading plan and stayed with it. By my count, I only missed seven days. I learned a lot, went on three short-term mission trips, and attended theology and apologetics classes at my church. I was growing spiritually and memorized the book of Philippians. The repetition required for that meant scripture was on my mind multiple times each day. I also began praying and talking to God throughout the day as well. It started feeling like a relationship, where we got to know one another. However, I wondered if I was right in believing that Someone was actually hearing me, since there was no concrete proof—only mere faith. I investigated other religions (honestly hoping to land in expectation-free atheism) but none offered the proof I sought.

Since I had no proof of an alternative, I tentatively continued my Christian walk, attending a Christian college, and of course telling nobody my intellect was pushing me away from faith. I read a physics book that explains how the universe came to be, but each book admitted to not knowing from where the laws of physics came. That doesn't mean there is no explanation. I knew that even if there were no alternatives, the chance of a fully satisfying life (and afterlife) was still worth putting my faith in Jesus. That deduction could determine my choice, but it does not prove truthfulness. It also makes sense that if a loving God exists and there was no proof, then God would come to us and ask us to believe in faith. This is what we see in Jesus but expecting something to be true does not make it true. I skeptically continued on in the privacy of my own mind, knowing that all my family and close friends were believers that I wanted to continue respecting me.

I graduated with degrees in math and economics, entering the workforce within a year. I got a good job at a great company in the financial industry and began wondering what I desired my life's work to accomplish. Predictably, contemplating ultimate significance while staring outside brought my mind to Jesus. I decided to do what I loved best: learning and thinking logically. I read a variety of books and one of them finally gave me the answer I was seeking. Lee Strobel's Case for Christ argues that if we attempt to study history at all, we must accept that Jesus of Nazareth lived, died on the cross, and rose from the grave. There is simply no other way to consistently study history beyond a few centuries ago.

Confidently satisfied with my quest for truth, I was faced with the question, "Now what?" What should I do with my life now that I'm all in? I already determined nothing except Jesus leads to a satisfying life of significance. Then, after spending time in prayer and thoughtful reflection on my experience, I understood that there isn't anything specific that I must accomplish to be a follower of Jesus. After all, the gospel is the good news about what Jesus did in the past! Once again, I was overthinking.

For in the Bible, Ephesians 2:8 says: "For it is by grace you have been saved, through faith—and this is not from yourselves, it is the gift of God." All I must do is walk humbly with my Lord, knowing He is Risen indeed!

Samuel Stewart

My name is Samuel Stewart, and my home is in Wisconsin. I am a follower of Jesus who has a passion for understanding the world. I studied math and economics at Wheaton College in Illinois and now work in the financial industry, of course in addition to my writing.

13

Good Enough

▼

by Ruth Ann Gumm

Adopted at nine weeks old into a Christian home, I have attended church all of my life. Every Sunday morning, we went to Sunday school and church. When I was 11, I felt convicted that I needed to be baptized to wash away my sins and insure my salvation. Prior to baptism, I felt dark and dirty, unworthy to be loved by God because of the sins I had committed. When I came up out of the baptismal waters, I saw a very bright light and felt completely clean. I felt as though I had a supernatural strength to take on the world. My experience matched squarely up with what I had been taught in church. From that point forward, when I prayed, I felt like God heard me. I had received the gift of the Holy Spirit that day. What I did with that gift and how I allowed the Holy Spirit to transform my life would come much later.

For years I struggled with the legalism of my actions being what saved me, as if I could earn salvation by an action that I took, by being good enough. It was many years later that I learned I was "good enough," because of the sacrifice of Jesus. God's one and only, perfect Son, made me good enough. I am saved because God made a way for me to be saved.

The fact that my adoptive father died young, complicated my emotional soul search and faith journey. My mother never re-married because she "didn't think anyone else would love us as much as she did." I was the only daughter. My twin brothers had each other, and my mom and I had each other. She and I were extremely close. Growing up, I was "the good child." I remember feeling an extreme pressure to just be good. My brothers caused stress in my family, while I was a source of peace for my mother. I vividly believed that my mom couldn't handle any additional stress beyond what my brothers already gave her.

The extreme pressure to be good led me to become a perpetual overachiever. Becoming the valedictorian of my class in high school is an example of how driven I felt all the time. When I found myself facing a divorce after 17 years of marriage, this was my first big life failure! My "good girl" image of myself was shaken to its core. The scriptures said God didn't like divorce. Wanting to please God, too, it was at this point that I really started talking to God, praying to Him for guidance, and studying scripture. It took the failure of my marriage to turn my dependence to God instead of myself. God began his ingraining of Romans 8:28 into my heart and mind, at that point in my life. When I look back over my life, every event leads up to the strong faith and dependence I have upon Him.

Multiple times in my life, I felt like my faith was weak; my faith in God; in Jesus and in my salvation. Every time, without exception, that I prayed for stronger faith, my God delivered! Plus, He delivered in a big way! He has protected my children from harm. He has allowed me to understand and speak a foreign language while on the mission field. He has reunited me with my birth family after I had been told I would never find them. He gave me peace about situations when there was no reason to have peace.

The moment that truly galvanized my faith was an encounter with a demon possessed woman. When that demon looked me in the eye and told me my faith wasn't strong enough to remove him, I knew that Jesus was strong enough. If that demon existed, which it clearly did, then everything else in the Bible was true as well. If God can use an evil beyond measure to bring someone to Him, there is nothing He can't use to develop and increase faith.

Our God is a mighty Father, and He answers the prayers of His children. We only need to ask for what we need and allow Jesus to make us GOOD ENOUGH!

Ruth Ann Gumm

Ruth Ann is mother to two lovely young women and bonus mom to beautiful twin daughters. She is a retired technology teacher, cheerleading coach, and FCA (Fellowship of Christian Athletes) sponsor. Her interests include her precious grandson, gardening, serving on medical missions, and leading Bible study. She is an active member of her church. Along with her husband, Steve, Ruth Ann resides in the Commonwealth of Kentucky.

14

From a Hurting Heart

▼

by Brooke Dobi-Strauss

It was in the early 1980s when I was nine or ten years old. I used to sit in my red carpeted bedroom in our house in our small town and just talk to someone (in my head). I didn't know who I was talking to, but I just felt a presence, I guess. My family was Jewish, but they were far from spiritual. We went to synagogue twice during the year and followed some of the holidays, but no one in my family ever talked about God or prayer. When I was a teenager, I always thought it was strange how Jews would sing Hebrew songs in synagogue but never really knew the meanings. When we were in synagogue or following certain traditions on holidays, it just seemed like they were going through the motions. If you asked an adult, "Why are we doing this?" they would give a speech about Jewish tradition. Sadly, this just never got into my heart. I didn't understand it and it felt like something was missing. I felt like the black sheep of my family.

My parents divorced when I was in the fourth grade. My mother was not a loving type of person. She was impatient from the day I was born. I never got the security or love I needed from her. As a young adult I realized she was quite emotionally abusive. When I was 13, my mother met a man who was from Montreal, Canada. One day she told my sister and me that she had some news. It was summer and she told us that she was getting remarried, so in December we were going to move to Montreal. She had just met him so needless to say, we burst into tears. I asked her, "What state is Montreal in?" Yes, I actually asked her that. Americans back then were not taught anything about our friendly Northern neighbor. She then explained that it was in another country called Canada.

It was extremely traumatic leaving our dad, grandparents and friends, and moving to a strange new place where they spoke another language. Things didn't go very well. Adjusting was difficult. I would hear my mother and stepfather arguing about his family. Sometimes I'd hear my stepfather yelling on the phone with his ex-wife. It was an unhappy situation. They got divorced after four years, but we stayed in Montreal because it had eventually become our home. Then my mother's abuse got worse. I got yelled at and was interrogated almost daily just because I was making friends of different races. She wanted to know why I was not making more Jewish friends. She was always edgy and took it out on me.

As time went on, I felt alone and unsupported. My sister and mother ganged up on me constantly. I began having anxiety attacks at 19.

One day, my mother admitted that she was not the best mother. She said that I had to go to therapy and pick up the pieces on my own. That was hard to hear. I had reached my early 20s and I had such a hunger for love, acceptance, and peace.

One day I met a man who told me about Jesus and how He died for my sins. At first it seemed so foreign because I had never learned anything about Him. But I was curious. The first time I stepped into a church, I cried. I remember crying and saying to myself, "What am I doing here? This is crazy! I'm a Jewish girl!" Deep down, however, I knew it felt right. When I told my family that I had accepted Christ and was now a Christian, they thought it was very strange, but I didn't care. I felt like I finally had some peace and real love.

Now at age 45, I am married and raising our 7 year old daughter in the church. We pray together and she believes in God. It's amazing to raise her in a spiritual household. Looking back, I can see how our Heavenly Father always had His mighty hand on me. I believe without a doubt that He is the one I was talking to as a child. I just didn't know Him yet.

Jewish parents give their children a Hebrew name at birth. Mine was "Bracha" which means blessing. Little did I know that the pain I experienced was a blessing in disguise as it led me to the Lord.

Brooke Dobi-Strauss

I live on the East coast with my hubby and young daughter. I have a virtual assistant business. I help business owners with tech and social media management. I am excited to share my unique testimony with others and hope that it may bring some people to Christ.

15

Seek and You Shall Find

▼

by Karen Glass

When I was 26 years old, I became very involved in church activities. I thought if I was going to invest my life serving God, I should know for sure that He is real. I started reading the Bible for myself for over two years, searching to know Him personally. A verse I learned as a child kept me searching. "Ask and it shall be given you, seek, and ye shall find, knock, and it shall be opened unto you." I noticed certain characters in the Bible had close relationships with God, and that's what I wanted. To me, He seemed very far away.

After two years of reading the Bible, I felt I was no closer to God than when I started. He still seemed distant. I spoke to Him aloud one day and said, "I kept my end of the bargain. I asked, sought, and I knocked, but haven't found you. If you are real, you must reveal yourself to me. The ball's in your court. I'm not reading the Bible anymore."

After about two weeks, I was dusting my family room with the television on for background noise. The 700 Club was on and a man said you could have a personal relationship with God. What is preventing it is your sin. I knew that Jesus paid for my sin on the cross, so why was He still so far away from me? The man went on to say that since Jesus rose from the dead and He was a living God, that I could call out to God. I could ask Him to forgive me of my sins. He would hear me and save me.

He quoted these verses: "The word is near you, even in your mouth and in your heart, that is the word of faith. That if you will confess with your mouth the Lord Jesus and will believe in your heart that God has raised Him from the dead, you will be saved. For with the heart man believes unto righteousness and with the mouth confession is made unto salvation. For whosoever calls on the name of the Lord shall be saved."

I figured I had nothing to lose, so right there in my family room, I got on my knees and told God I knew I was a sinner. I asked Him to come into my life and save me.

I stood up thinking nothing happened, because there was no feeling, no bells or whistles to signify He heard me or answered me. I thought, "Oh well, at least I tried again."

As time went on, I began to notice changes coming from within me. If I would swear, I felt really awful about it. I also was set free from a habit I had been powerless to break before I prayed that prayer. I started reading the Bible again and the words seemed to be written to me, now. They weren't just information on a page. I started changing from within.

A couple of weeks had passed when my husband's co-worker's wife invited me to a Bible study. I went and relayed how I had prayed and asked God to save me. They all looked knowingly at me and explained how they, too, had asked God to save them from their sins. They told me I was, what the Bible calls, "born-again." They said the changes that I was experiencing were evidence of the Holy Spirit indwelling me. I have been walking with Jesus ever since and loving Him!

Karen Glass

Karen lives with Phil, her husband of 44 years. They have two sons, two daughters-in-love, and eight grands. She and her sister care for their elderly mother between their two homes. Karen is active in biking and hiking. Karen and Phil have pedaled 1,300 miles on their tandem bicycle. They hike regularly on the Ice Age Trail in Wisconsin where they reside. They are enjoying retirement.

16

Turning My Mess into My Message

▼

by Kristyn Schott

My first semester of college (as a college athlete) I was finally on fire for God. Then my second semester hit, as did my eating disorder, and I fell the furthest away from God I've ever been.

Let me rewind a bit. I grew up believing in God, but what I had in belief, I lacked in faith. So, while I knew who God and Jesus were, I didn't know them as part of a personal relationship. Part of me thought God loved me because I was such a "good" kid. In high school, I finally came to realize God loved me for me, because of Christ, and nothing I did. While I found myself letting go of my pessimism and constant worrying about the future, I still lacked that personal relationship.

That is until my first semester of college when I met my best friend (who also came to Christ that semester) and we burned bright for God. Coming down from the high of my first semester of college and how on fire I was for God, I crashed hard in my second semester as I fell deep into my eating disorder, and consequently, deeply away from God. Second semester of college, I felt God slip away. I was angry, confused, and upset. Why would He do that? Well, of course, I now know that it wasn't Him who fell away but me, because I was trapped in my eating disorder.

I idolized food (or lack thereof), calories, my body, and exercise as I moved from Anorexia or Orthorexia and deeper into the lies and rituals of my eating disorder. During this time, I gave up on God, but God never gave up on me. It's only by His grace that I escaped that dark place.

My senior year of college I broke my rib playing in one of our volleyball games. God used the moment that broke me (literally and figuratively) to point me to recovery and back to Him. From that moment, I threw myself into seeking God – whether through the Bible, church, worship music, or praying. It was a long and hard road, not only recovering from my eating disorder but also restoring my relationship with God. I wanted to find the freedom that I so desperately craved.

But here I am, three years later, and I'm nowhere near the place of being on fire for God like I was that first semester...I'm actually much further along. What I thought was a fire was just a simple candle, and now I have a bonfire burning bright for God.

Through that process, God truly turned my mess into my message. Now I live to tell the world about the freedom and the hope God can provide to everyone. He brought me out of that dark space so that He could send me back into the hole to shine the light of Christ to help others get out, too. That led me to writing More Than Conquerors, a devotional for girls and women who have struggled or are struggling with an eating disorder.

It's crazy to look back where I was in high school (before

having a personal relationship with God), that first semester of college (feeling like I was on fire), my eating disorder (furthest from God), and compare it to today. The difference is unbelievable, and it was only made possible by Christ. Today, I'm passionate about sharing my story, God's goodness and grace, and the truth that we were created to live for more than this world tells us.

Kristyn Schott

Hey y'all, I'm Kristyn—an author, copywriter and founder of Created for More ministry from the great state of Texas. My goal in life is to help people take hold of faith, pursue purpose, and become all they were created to be in God. In my free time, I love to read, play the piano, and spend time with friends and family.

17

The Rainbow that Made Me Dream

▼

by Marina Maria

There is nothing wrong with dreaming after you've read about a rainbow, is there? At age eight, I will never forget how reading my best friend's poem, *Rainbow*, started my dream journey. It made me forget about my colorless surroundings and the harsh, dark realities of my childhood. I wanted to have a rainbow life filled with laughter and those dolls that I always desired for playtime, the clothes that I wanted to wear to look pretty and polished, and plenty of food. I wanted to wake up in the morning and be able to eat a big breakfast and take a full lunch bag to school. After reading the rainbow poem, I began to pick up my pencil daily to write in my diary. The rainbow made me temporarily smile, even when I did not have God in my life. I imagined that someday I would have a house that would not be an embarrassment. It hid the confusion and anger that the horrible sexual abuse caused in me. With my pencil, I could transform the darkness in my life to light by using bright or colorful words, when there was very little to eat at home or when I witnessed my mother suffer domestic violence. The rainbow kept me dreaming of painting my life with more colors instead of one color. For many years until adulthood, I kept a journal of my feelings and experiences. Later I wrote poetry and short stories to recreate my life with my pencil.

Growing up in Lansing, Michigan was challenging. I endured the winter weather with my four sisters and seven brothers. Many times, our heat broke down or was turned off in the middle of winter. Nights when it was below zero are when I felt the coldest physically and emotionally. I slept with my sisters who became my heated blanket. Hugging them warmed me and enabled my heart to dream more. My sister, Julieta, became my surrogate mother and helped my biological mother take care of me. Other older sisters and brothers took care of the younger ones, too. Without God in my life, I had to learn to trust the world. This was painful, but my journal dream writing continued.

After college graduation, I moved to Redondo Beach, California where I started working and met my first husband. We were married for 11 years. During my marriage, I still had unforgiveness in my life toward the men who had sexually abused me. Because of this, I went through an identity crisis, which led to a divorce, when combined with my unforgiveness. The rainbow in my mind was colorless at this time. I thought that obtaining a master's degree in Mexican American studies would help me find my true Mexican American identity, but it did not. I searched for God in the wrong places, from the wrong men, and from the wrong people. I became involved in false religions and with false gods. That left me even emptier. I continued to write in my journal, but the gloomy words I used created grey clouds instead of blue skies.

One night, when I was tired of being bitter, I prayed to God to send me a man that He had chosen for my life. A few weeks later, I met my husband, Louie. I was working at my new job as an online Academic Counselor for an online university. Louie was finishing his bachelor's degree at the same university. I was his Academic Counselor. After three years of a long-distance friendship, we were married. During this time, I began my elementary school teaching career with my husband's encouragement. During the third year of our long-distance friendship, he came to visit me and led me to Christ on Easter Sunday. We walked up a golf course hill together. I peacefully sat down on the grass beside Louie. Yes, I was ready to accept Jesus. I repented of all my sins and felt a weight lift off of me. Louie said the words of the sinner's prayer for me. I closed my eyes and repeated them.

When I opened my eyes, I immediately saw the world in beautiful, vivid rainbow colors. I felt the Lord's eternal peace. At that moment, the peace that surpasses all understanding was given to me. My dark clouds were gone, and light filled my life. I finally discovered that my true identity is in Christ Jesus. After accepting Christ into my life, a new rainbow appeared across the sky of my mind. I could dream again. I finally felt ready to fulfill God's purpose for my life. That Resurrection Sunday, I was made new in Him. I am now living a genuinely colorful, rainbow-filled life for Him.

Marina Maria

Marina Maria has been an elementary school teacher for 16 years in Arizona. In her free time, she interviews Christian pastors and leaders to share their testimonies and to discuss the gospel on her global internet radio program, Faith City Outreach, which airs on Evangelism Radio. Marina lives with her husband, Louie, in Glendale, Arizona, where they enjoy cycling together. They have two children.

18

Calling Us Home

▼

by Heather Browne

I was born into a family that lived fractured and confused in spirituality and in mind. My mother was a paranoid schizophrenic. That meant my young years were often consumed with trying to help her feel safe. My sister escaped into alcohol and boys' arms. Dad, overwhelmed, worked long and hard hours to keep my Mom home versus locked away in an institution from all of us.

God was not really mentioned as prayers seemed frivolous when we were more concerned with the hallucinations heard and Mom's rampant fear. Somehow, I still knew there was a God and that He was full of love.

My mother killed herself when I was 16. Our family crumbled even farther apart. I knew I needed a family, one different than mine. Somehow, once again, I knew I needed to go to church.

The first one I attempted along with my Dad, had us wear huge pins announcing we were guests. I enjoyed the music and the church, but as we packed up to leave, no one came to say hello. I knew this was not to be a new home for me, so I never returned.

I asked friends at school if they attended church. One warmly invited me. I eagerly went and was quickly embraced and offered kindness and space. I became actively involved in that church and joined the high school group and the choir.

When I went off to college, I found a huge church, but found myself wrestling with the truth that my mother might not be in Heaven. I met with the pastor and shared that I had read the Bible, knew what was shared, but struggled that God would be so cold as to not see my mother's mental illness. The pastor shared that she was clearly in hell and that I needed to accept this. The presentation was cold and un-caring. I realized, of course, that this might be the truth, but for a man to tell me what God's judgement and heart was felt wrong. I pulled away from joining the church and I began exploring all religions.

I returned to my high school church following college and presented the same challenge to the pastor who shared this truth was knowledge between God and my mom. He asked if he could pray for my struggle with this. His warmth and compassion blessed me deeply. He became an important part of my walk.

I began dating and met the man I would wed. I asked if we could go to his church, as he had not been attending in a few years. We began our walk of faith together. During our dating I knew I wanted my life to be with God and asked Jesus into my heart. We lived a life together as husband and wife and raised our kids for 20 years. I homeschooled so I could share faith freely. We were active in leadership at church.

The church offered an office so I could counsel the church members. I am a faith-based psychotherapist.

Surprisingly, poetry started to come to me suddenly the year before my husband died. I was quickly published and often. When my husband suddenly died, I was already established as a poet. I began writing on grief and these moments with God, too. I now see that this was God's hand preparing me to write non-fiction and fiction as well. I am grateful that I continue to find places of publication in *Psychology Today*, *Focus on the Family*, *Bethlehem Writer's Circle*, etc. I have won several awards and been nominated for the Pushcart for poetry. My hope is to help others grow and heal.

Dr. Heather Browne

Dr. Heather Browne is an internationally award-winning poet, author, and faith-based psychotherapist. Heather loves to encourage others to choose to live their life full of awe, joy, creativity and love. She has appeared and been interviewed on ABC7 News and KDOC.

19

I Am a Leaner

▼

by Nyla Kay Wilkerson

I grew up in a Christian home. My extended family were church goers. For a young midwestern girl, I thought this was the normal life. Sunday mornings were a happy time filled with gospel music playing on the television while we dressed in our best for church. Songs from what now is called Children's Church are embedded deep within my heart. My nieces, nephew, and grandchildren learned For God So Loved the World; Climb, Climb up Sunshine Mountain; and Deep and Wide, while I rocked them.

When I was 12, my daddy had a fatal heart attack, at home, at the tender age of 37. I remember it to this day. The sight, sound, and pain are permanently engraved in my memory. My maternal grandmother was living with us at that time. She was small in stature, but mighty in faith. Immediately, we prayed for God to heal and help. My mother came home from work just as the emergency workers were taking my father out on a gurney, feverishly working to revive him.

When we got to the hospital, we were informed Daddy had died on the way there. He'd had a massive heart attack. My world changed in that instant. Devastated, I questioned why God did not answer our prayers and save Daddy. I had a 5 year old sister. What would we do without him? My grandmother assured me that God always had a plan that would turn everything into good. I did not believe her. There was no good in this.

My paternal grandparents lived 90 minutes away. They had come up for the weekend and we had an exceptionally nice time. I remember watching them playing Canasta and listening to their laughter. They even extended their visit. The next day they lost their only son. Looking back, I can see what a gift God gave them. The gift of time and memories before they were separated from their son was better than any material gift they had ever received. God knows what we need and gives it abundantly.

A few months later, a Christian college was having a revival in our church. They were looking for families to host the kids. Since I had been questioning God not loving me, my mother signed up to house a girl. Julie was on fire for God. We talked a long time. She asked me to go each of the nights to listen to their music and message. My family and I did. When we returned home, Julie would answer questions and tell me stories of her life. I expected it to be perfect, but that was far from true. She explained how sometimes bad things happen to good people. That is when we lean in closer to God instead of stepping away from Him, which I had been doing—stepping away.

On the last night, I remember the invitation hymn, Just as I Am, and the feel of my hymnal in my hands. As I began singing, I felt a hand on my shoulder and another one guide my hand to close the songbook. I looked over, but no one was there. The hand pressed on my back. I edged out of the pew to the altar, followed by my mother and grandmother. I knelt and gave my heart to Jesus.

The feeling was unlike anything I had experienced. My entire body was warmed. Joy filled my heart and soul. I was His, forgiven, and forever loved. Just going to church is nothing compared to giving your heart to the Savior. God used my broken heart and a young college girl to draw me to Him. I started truly living for Him that day and I haven't stopped. My life has not been lived perfectly, but it has been lived for Him. Since I have become a leaner instead of a stepper, I have been much more at peace.

Nyla Kay Wilkerson

Nyla Kay Wilkerson is a follower of Jesus and prayer warrior. A retired Christian bookstore owner and upper elementary Sunday School teacher, she now reviews books, writes a Christian blog, Abba's Prayer Warrior Princess abbasprayer-warriorprincess@wordpress.com, co-blogs on Heart Wings Blog heartwingsblog.com, and is writing a novel. She has published one cookbook. Hobbies include cooking, gardening, and antiques. She resides in Indiana with her husband and two pets, a Siamese and Pekeapoo.

20

My Best Yes

▼

by Sarah Rivera

I suffered from rejection at a very early age. The family that I knew was torn apart by divorce. My whole life was completely shattered at the age of five. I remember that day like it was yesterday. The events of that day and the day prior are still so clear in my mind. I remember my dad breaking the news to me as I was sitting next to my mom on the couch. He said, "I'm going to go stay with Grandma for a while." It felt like an eternity before he spoke again. He then continued, "I need to get going before she locks the door on me."

I was a young child, whose heart was broken for the very first time and all I could muster up to say was, "I hate you!"

Time went on. I was trying to grasp how to properly live two separate lives. The hurt, the pain, the rejection, and the abandonment I was allowing to well up inside me caused me to become an angry, bitter child. I was filled with unforgiveness and rage. I kept everyone far away, protecting myself, so no one could get close enough to hurt me again. My mom started to attend a Christian church with my sister and me a few months after the divorce. It was at that church that I accepted Christ as my Lord and Savior, around the age of nine. I, unfortunately, didn't really know what that meant. I just thought it was a cool thing to do because the other kids in my Sunday school class were doing it. I guess that was a good form of peer pressure.

Fast forward to my teenage years, I've now, like many people, walked away from my faith. I was still experiencing the anger and bitterness about the hurt I endured as a child. I met a boy in my early twenties and we quickly started to date. After about a year, we ended up moving in together. I thought this was it. He was going to be the man with whom I would spend the rest of my life. There were red flags in the beginning of our relationship. I ignored those signs because I wanted so deeply to be loved and find my forever person. We unknowingly allowed our issues from the past to creep into our relationship. The baggage we carried around with us included hurt, fear, anxiety, and depression. Boy, was there a lot of depression! A relationship with two hurting people wasn't healthy. That unhealthiness cut so deep it came out of our pores.

January 2017 was when he decided that he could no longer be in a relationship with me. That is when my world shattered for a second time. My dad didn't want me and now the man I thought I was going to marry didn't want me either. That same month, I dropped onto my living room floor, weeping. I was texting my mom and my cousin. They were both reminding me of Jesus and how much He loved me. At that moment, a sudden peace came over me. It was something I've never before experienced. I was still on the same living room floor, I was still at the beginning of heartbreak, I had the same tear residue falling down my face, but I was at peace; a peace that only God can provide.

I started praying to God that very same night. I recommitted my life to Jesus Christ a few weeks later and never looked back. I got baptized in April 2018 and I am now working at my home church, feeling a strong call to ministry. I am working towards my bachelor's degree in Christian Leadership with a minor in Church Ministries. My life isn't perfect, but I am progressing and being obedient to God's call. Did I enjoy the pain I endured during the past three years of healing and counseling? Absolutely not. Am I enjoying basking in God's love for me and experiencing a freedom only He can provide? You know it! Saying yes to God was by far my best yes.

Sarah Rivera

I was born and raised in Milwaukee, WI with a strong prayer that the Lord will take me to a warmer location! I enjoy making people laugh and doing what I can to best serve them in different seasons of life. I love Jesus and will never regret saying yes to Him!

21

Why I Am a Christian

▼

by James C. Koenig

My journey to becoming a Christian has been a circuitous one. I was raised in a "Christian" home, with my mother dragging us kids to church each Sunday, while my father slept. I went to church reluctantly, and as a result, my mind was not receptive to the message.

When I began college, I did not know if God existed. I saw all the evil and calamities in the world, and I wondered how a "loving" God could allow such things to happen. I was convinced there was a devil, but I was uncertain about God.

I met a godly woman in 1980 and started attending the same church as her entire family. I really began to search the scriptures and, for the first time, hear the message of the Gospel. I was still a skeptic and needed a lot of proof before I could truly believe in a loving God. Consequently, I began my personal search for God. I read the entire Bible. I checked out countless books from the library. I looked into Eastern religion and I researched Islam and Judaism. I stayed up reading long into the night, searching for the answer to my ultimate question: "If there is a God, who is He?"

I found the Eastern faiths were more about a philosophy than a god. After reading a bit of the Quran and finding it disjointed and indecipherable, I discarded these and concentrated on Judaism and Christianity. I became absorbed in the Torah, the first five books of the Bible, and then the stories about Saul, David, Solomon, and the kings that followed. The entire Old Testament looked forward to the coming Messiah, to right wrongs and bring justice to a world that seemingly had no eternal justice.

After reading the New Testament, I became convinced that if Jesus was indeed the long-awaited Jewish Messiah, then He was also God. Jesus said that the only proof He would provide was the sign of Jonah—that He would be killed, spend three days and three nights in the tomb, and then be resurrected back to life. Thus, the focus of my search became at long last, a study of the life of Jesus and most importantly, did He actually rise from the dead? I came to realize that all of Christianity rested on the supposition that Jesus was crucified, died, and then rose from the dead. If Jesus actually lived (and was not just a myth) and if He did indeed rise from the dead, then I could finally admit I'd found my answers.

I began an intensive historical search about Jesus. I learned that several extra-biblical sources acknowledged that Jesus had actually lived and was crucified by Pontius Pilate. Having established Jesus as a historical personage, the only question that remained was whether He rose from His grave. I found the answers to my question in the Josh McDonald book, More Than A Carpenter (1977 edition). In this well-researched book, I found compelling evidence that Jesus did indeed rise from the dead, thus proving His Deity.

Satisfied that I'd found the true God, I was baptized on Easter Sunday in 1981. Convinced I'd found my Savior, I then sought answers to the other great question: "Why does an all-powerful God allow so much evil in this world?" Once again, I perused many library volumes on Christian apologetics, searching for answers. In Norman Geisler's book, *I Don't Have Enough Faith to Be an Atheist*, I found that the world is what it is because of our sin. I came to realize that if God wanted to eliminate evil in this world, He would have to eliminate the very people He created and loved, for we are the source of evil in this world. It was then that I realized the extent of my own sin and how mankind's disobedience to God is the root of evil in our world. Instead of pointing the finger of accusation against God, I found that it was me who was at fault. I needed the Savior's blood to atone for my sin and the sins of the world.

I still have many questions about God, and I realize that on this side of heaven, I will not find answers to all of my questions. However, I found the answers to the key questions about God, and since then, I have given my life over to the Savior.

James C. Koenig

Jim is 65 years old, has been married for 30 years, and is the father of 6 children. He is a dentist by profession, but has a wide range of interests, including photography, Christian apologetics, reading, writing, fishing, hiking, and traveling. He lives in rural Forest Lake, Minnesota.

22

Your Past Does Not Determine Your Future

▼

by Leslie Nafus

The Early Days

I am the sixth of six children in my family. My nearest sibling is seven years older than me. I spent the bulk of my early childhood alone at home with my mother. Mr. Rogers was my best friend. I loved lying on my back under the maple tree in our backyard looking at the blue, blue sky through the green, green leaves, just thinking. When I was seven, shortly after my parents built their "dream home," they began to have marital trouble. My father became openly unfaithful to my mother. My mother returned the favor and found another man. They separated for a time but then decided to resolve things and reconcile. They planned a large family dinner to announce their decision, bring the family back together, and celebrate the reunion.

My mother and I left for the store to pick up some last-minute items for dinner. However, instead of going to the store, we met the man she was having an affair with at a fleabag motel. He told her to "get rid" of me. So, my mother drove me to an acquaintance's house and left me on her front porch, supposedly so she could run errands. That was the last time I saw my mother until I was much, much older. Many decades passed without a phone call, a birthday or Christmas card, or even a note to stay in touch.

Later On

After my mother's abandonment, my father moved the woman he'd been having an affair with into our "dream home." We had very regularly gone to church all of my life. My father even helped build the church we attended. I had heard about Jesus, how to get saved, and the stories of the

Bible every Sunday at church. They were part of the background fabric of my life. When the church leaders learned of my father's situation, they asked him to step down from any service positions he worked in for the church. They asked the woman who would become my stepmother to also step down from the ministries in which she participated.

We sold the "dream house" and moved to the next town over, where my father's business concerns were. He was a successful entrepreneur in financial planning and life insurance as well as a restauranteur. It was in this new town that I had my first experience with public school. Unfortunately, it was awful. In the Christian school I had attended since kindergarten, I was ostracized for my parents' behavior. The teachers and students at the public school, on the other hand, hated me for having been a "private school kid." School went from an unpleasant experience to a nightmare for me.

This was true of life in general. My stepmother was more of a step-monster and her son...well, he began to abuse me sexually. Then came the big move. My father uprooted our whole lives and moved us to northern North Idaho, where I finished my growing up years in the woods, twenty miles from the nearest town. It was in this community that I met Jesus when

I was 15 and began attending a non-denominational, charismatic church. I got baptized and was filled with the Holy Spirit.

I want to tell you life got a whole lot better after that, but that would be untrue. Even though I loved Jesus and believed He loved me, I didn't fit into that church. I left my father's house, got a job, and moved in with my sister, her husband, and two children. I put myself through the rest of high school and looked forward to college. Instead of college, I met a predator in church who was quite a lot older than me and married him. I thought that would fix things and I would finally have a place to belong as well as a family of my own. Instead, it was a 21-year unmitigated domestic violence disaster.

Today

But God is merciful. I found a counselor in 1998 who relentlessly pursued my healing under the direction of the Holy Spirit for more than two decades. Through this, I was able to heal spiritually and physically. I graduated from college with honors and a bachelor's degree in Liberal Arts in 2006, fulfilling a lifelong dream and calling. In 2007, I divorced my abusive husband, moved to Maui, Hawaii, and began healing in earnest with Jesus by my side every step of the arduous journey. I started a gluten-free bakery that quickly became successful, serving clients like Wolfgang Puck's Spago Maui restaurant and other high-end clientele. I became a certified SCUBA diver, fulfilling another lifelong dream. Today, I am a professional marketing copywriter, a #1 International Amazon Bestselling Author, happily married to a good husband, and founder of the 68:11 Collective, a group dedicated to activating 1 million women (& discerning men) into entrepreneurship and financial freedom.

What can Jesus do? ANYTHING with a life surrendered to Him.

Leslie Nafus

Leslie Nafus is an international bestselling author, professional copywriter, speaker, coach, lifelong entrepreneur, and founder of the 68:11 Collective that teaches women to become better entrepreneurs by giving them the foundational skills they need to start and grow a successful business. Learn more at www.leslienafus.com.

23

Jesus: My American Dream

▼

by Laura Barker

What is the "American Dream"? I suppose it is slightly different for everyone. Essentially, it is fall in love, get married, buy a house, have two to four children, live a quiet life, and die happy at a ripe old age, surrounded by the people you love. That has probably been the basic dream of humans all over this world for thousands of years. Unfortunately for most of us, that is not the way life works out.

I was born at the very end of the baby-boom in Milwaukee, Wisconsin. Yes, I'm a mid-western baby boomer. I was the middle child of three, with a typical middle-child personality, trying to get attention in any way I could. I had as happy a childhood as anyone else. I lived pretty much like everyone else, but for some reason that I don't understand and am forever grateful, Jesus picked me to be one of His own.

Cathy was my best friend growing up. Her parents were Dutch immigrants to America, and born-again Christians. Over the many years of our friendship, I had a multitude of sleepovers at Cathy's house. Every time I was there, her mom talked to me about Jesus. It was very casual, not preachy. She was just living the Christian life out loud.

I was included in countless of their family activities. I tagged along with Cathy to Christian youth rallies, Bible studies, and to her church on Sunday mornings. As a teenager at one of the youth rallies, the words the speaker uttered shot straight to my heart. I clearly understood that I was a sinner in need of a savior. They called for anyone who wanted to give their life to Jesus to come forward—I did. Then a few months later the Billy Graham Crusade made a stop in Milwaukee, and I went forward for salvation there, too. I was really good at "getting saved," but I wasn't so good at the follow-through afterwards. So, what did I do? I slowly or in some cases quickly went back to just living that common American lifestyle. I entered a time of rebellion.

The decade of the 1980s was my rebellious period. I partied and lived together with a man I barely knew. He introduced me to drugs, some of which I tried, and beat me sometimes, not exactly the dream my parents envisioned for me. I lived in Memphis, Tennessee for three years, then we moved to Reno, Nevada. I worked as a bartender and later as a blackjack dealer in a casino. After being in Reno for a couple of years I finally told that guy to hit the road. It was a hard time in my life, but it was perfect timing for Jesus to remind me of His love and that He never left my side during all those years. A friend and coworker invited me to join her at a new church, and I happily went.

I was emotionally messed up and so ready to jump back into Jesus' arms. I knew Him, and He already knew me. It didn't take long for me to re-dedicate my life to Jesus. I knew I was already saved, but it just didn't look very much like I was. What I was missing was discipleship. I needed to learn what it meant to be a Christian—to make Jesus Lord of my life, how to study the Bible, and to pray. Jesus knew exactly what I needed, because that church founded a place that was somewhat comparable to a sorority house. They called it the "Women's Discipleship House." I happily moved in and lived with a few other young women along with a slightly older woman who was our mentor, friend, and spiritual mother. She taught us all how to pray, to love ourselves and others as Jesus loves, how to worship and be humble, and have a heart full of gratitude. My spirit grew in that house in Reno. I was baptized in a backyard hot tub and fell in love with Jesus in Reno.

It has been many years since I moved back to Milwaukee, 30 in fact. I've lived a lot, made mistakes, and have had many heartaches but many more joys. Through all of that, Jesus has never given up on me. I still cling to him with my whole heart and strength because I know that without Jesus this life has no meaning, no purpose, and no peace. The marriage, the house, the two to four children, and dying at a ripe old age doesn't mean anything without Jesus. Living for Jesus and loving Him is my calling, my adventure, and my American Dream.

Laura Barker

I am a mom to two adult daughters and "Grandma LaLa" to my darling granddaughter. And I can't leave out my big boy, Scout, a German Shepherd/Collie mix. I am happy that we all live near each other so we can get together often. I am a busy office manager at my church that currently has four locations. When I have free time, I enjoy reading, crafting, and watching British dramas. My life is never dull, and I wouldn't have it any other way.

24

With Christ, All Things Are Possible

▼

by Shonda Fischer

I grew up in a small town in Missouri in a very dysfunctional family. My home life consisted of mental abuse by a father who had lived it himself. Don't get me wrong, my dad was a good provider, but emotionally distant. My mother shouldered getting us to church and raising us to know God.

I accepted Christ when I was ten, but never really fed that relationship. Once I hit my teen years, I turned rebellious against my parents and all of their yelling, criticism, and lack of attention. I went out and lived my life, my way. I knew I didn't want to ruin my life by getting in trouble, so I made sure I had fun, but kept everything under control, or so I thought.

I married a boyfriend who all I really had in common with was partying. Our first year of marriage, I got pregnant and had a precious baby girl. I wanted to be a family that went on vacations together. I dreamed of being involved in all aspects of my child's life and doing this with a loving husband by my side. Unfortunately, things didn't go as planned.

Instead, I was married to a man who was an alcoholic, never spent time at home with his family, and was mentally abusive. I was divorced after three years of marriage. However, I was determined to have a good life for me and my daughter.

After dating and doing things without God, I soon fell into another serious relationship that was not only mentally abusive, but physically, as well. I was relieved by the fact that we were not married. I was emotionally spent, my life was miserable, and I had nowhere to turn. I was so desperate to get my life back on track. Fortunately, I knew I had to give it to God.

I literally fell on my knees in my living room and cried out to God to help me. I knew I couldn't fix me and had to relinquish control to the One who could. I gave my life to God, right then and there. A surreal peace enveloped me. I felt God's hand on my shoulder and heard His voice tell me that HE had great things for me. God was waiting on me to live for Him again and to give Him the control over my life.

Twenty-two years later, I'm married to a wonderful man, who is my equal partner in life. We have worked in children's ministry in our church for 17 years. My husband has helped me raise my daughter and our son to know and love God. We are a very close family and have been heavily involved in every aspect of our children's lives. My grown daughter is now in ministry herself and is on fire for our Savior. My son is attending college and still lives at home, attending church and living for God every day. Don't get me wrong, I still have trials. I just learned the hard way that without Christ I can't do anything, but with Christ all things are possible!

Shonda Czeschin Fischer

Shonda Czeschin Fischer is a wife and mother of two, who has been married for 21 years to her husband, Craig. She has worked alongside him in children's ministry for 17 years. Shonda loves reading, reviewing books and anything involving history. She resides in Missouri, where she spends time with her ShihTzu, Daisy, and Siamese cat, Nala. Shonda loves to talk about God. She enjoys encouraging and uplifting others.

25

Destined to Love Him

▼

by Aliza Mendoza, Associate Member

My belief in God is generational. My ancestors were forced into the Catholic religion and it continued within our culture, our heritage, all the way down to the moment I was born. I mention, specifically, the belief in God because although my parents chose to identify as Catholic, my father spoke of God as a universal being. That everyone's God was the same, they just interpreted His Word differently. Which is most definitely NOT Catholic tradition. Sure, we followed tradition in certain regards. I was baptized in the Catholic church, had my first communion, went to mass and church school. My father taught me the Bible, about its lessons and to make sure I did what is most important, to have faith.

Somewhere down the destructive path of my youth, I found myself asking the wrong questions and denying my faith as a form of rebellion against our Father. The in-fighting between religions, the politics, and all the misdeeds of man, I blamed on God. When in fact, this was not His way at all. The horror of terrorism, violence against people of color, how my ancestors were indoctrinated, made me angry and resentful. And then I became a mother. After a miscarriage and years of doctors telling me I would not be able to have children without a barrage of fertility treatments, and even then I might not carry to term, my child was born, and the realization dawned. He was always with me.

God gave me a purpose. Me, this seemingly lost and broken creature fumbling this planet, who has always felt inadequate inside and out. And yet, it is safe to say I was incredibly humbled by the gift. My daughter has taught me that I am hopelessly out of control, and that scares the life out of me. I want to protect her at any cost, but how would she ever reach her full potential if I kept her hidden away? It is one of my greatest fears that I struggle with every day.

I had never come to terms with the paradox of having free will and having our destinies pre-determined. What if I had been thrust into a life of misery? What if my father had not influenced me so? But to be near my daughter is to love her. She radiates joy and energy that could only be a blessing. I realized that He chose this life for me because I was strong enough to endure. I am hard working enough to not just survive but flourish. I am enough. I was predestined to love Him. My ancestors fought to survive to carry His word and the faith onto their children, as I will, without hesitation. In all my life I never thought to consider just how awesome that is.

Aliza Mendoza

My name is Aliza Mendoza. I have lived in the same midwestern city my entire life, but my parents are from Mexico. Being bilingual has helped me to land public services jobs that I've found fulfilling. I am a single mom of one amazing girl who has sparked my dream of working for NASA. I don't have a specific ministry that I represent as I am taking baby steps in my faith and loving God.

Note from the CWC's founder, Stephanie: Aliza is our only Associate Member (AM) featured in this book. As it says on our webpage about Associate Membership,

> The purpose of Associate Membership is to give people that are young chronologically and/or spiritually, the time, tools, and discipleship, they need to mature in Christ and as a writer.

We usually match an AM with one of our Standard Members willing to serve as their mentor. But we made an exception for Aliza's mentor. She is a Christian, married, mother of 3 children that were all under the age of 5 until her oldest turned 5 in August 2021. For now, her only CWC responsibility is to mentor Aliza.

To learn more about the benefits of becoming an Associate Member or a Mentor, visit the NEW! Associate Membership webpage of our website, www.christianwriterscollective.com.

26

Only Jesus Can Satisfy

▼

by Wm. David Waterman

The one thing that was typical of my existence before I became a Christian was that I was never satisfied. By the time I was 20 years old, I had worked in construction trades, had been a machinist, worked as a salesman, and I had tried several other careers. I would start out in each endeavor with great excitement and soon become bored. Having been blessed (or cursed) with a very active mind, I was continually experimenting, designing, and looking for things to do that would satisfy me.

Jesus Can...

We were poor and we understood that. But we also were dealing with major crises at home. Our father was not someone I could call "Dad" easily. He had a terrible temper and would often resort to hitting a child in the head or wherever he could connect when he wanted to punish. I was always trying hard to please my father. I saw it as a matter of survival and avoiding being beaten.

My mother was a huge contrast. She was open to anyone and tended to measure people by their character. Where my father would never forgive anyone, Mom would try to see things from the other person's point of view. Some people, however, even she never could tolerate.

I had been raised in church. My mother had us in church every Sunday. In the cold winter or the hot summer, it was a given that if my siblings and I weren't sick, we were going with her to church on Sunday.

It was in that small town Lutheran church in the Midwest that I was assured God was real. On one particular Sunday morning, while my mother was chatting with the pastor, I stepped back into the sanctuary and I felt Him. His Spirit still lingered there, even though the congregation had dispersed. The praise, singing, and message were all over, but

God was still there. So real was this feeling, it almost felt like I could reach out and touch Him. It seemed to me, that Sunday afternoon, that I could see a soft glow in the air as I looked toward the altar at the front of the pews.

A few years later, I was sleeping with my brother (big family means shared beds) when I was awakened by a brilliant white figure, who stood at the foot of the bed looking at me. No fear, just an incredible peace came over me as He moved from the foot of the bed, up to the head of the bed, laid His hand on me, and then disappeared. My brother was completely unaware of the event. When I shared the experience at the breakfast table, my father, who believed in extra-sensory perception (ESP) and read a lot of Edgar Cayce's and Jean Dixon's books, declared it was my deceased grandmother wanting to see me since she had passed away before we met.

My mother had waited to have us baptized. Instead of us three younger children being 'baptized' as infants, we were baptized after we made the decision to follow God and live for Him. I was baptized at age 13, and there He was again, standing there beside the pastor, smiling. Again, I felt that deep peace.

At age 15, I was beaten unconscious by my father because I collected an amount he considered insufficient for a service I had performed in my little shop. That beating and another head injury resulted in serious memory problems and some disability in my body. It also left me bitter.

Fast forward to my adult life...by the time I arrived in the sheep and cattle country of Colorado, I had regained considerable dexterity in my right hand and side. This made it possible for me to work at ranches. On December 23, 1980, everything changed.

I was invited to the church, in the village nearby, for Christmas dinner and evening services. After services, a young man shared his testimony and invited me to recommit to the Lord. As he shared his testimony of his salvation experience, there was that person again. He was reaching out toward me and gesturing for me to come to Him. I got out of the chair I was sitting in and threw the cigarettes in my pocket into the wood burning stove. Suddenly, I felt peace and joy that no words can describe. I went home, poured out the liquor in the cupboard, and was truly free of bitterness and hurt. I KNEW He was real. My life was forever changed. I have and always will serve Him.

Wm. David Waterman

Wm. David Waterman's life was dramatically changed just two days before Christmas in 1980. On that day, Jesus took his anger, bitterness, and dissatisfaction, and gave him indescribable peace and joy in return. Jesus also healed his addictions to cigarettes and alcohol on December 23, 1980. Today, he lives in New Mexico with his wife, Patti, and also serves as her caregiver.

27

Doing God's Business

▼

by Dana Williamson

Now faith is the substance of things hoped for, the evidence of things not seen. Hebrews 11:1

There is nothing too hard for God. Yet, it took me a while to realize, giving up what was in me, was allowing God to push me into greatness. Writing this testimony was extremely hard in order to share clearly, spiritually and effectively for you, the reader.

Follow me for a minute:

When I first started as an entrepreneur, it was because I wanted to be available for my children. All under 10 years of age at the time, I wanted to be there to drop them off at school, pick them up, help with homework, and cook a full meal every day. Those were my intentions, my goals.

It did not happen that way. I got tied up in a relationship where the other person did not understand the significance of having your own business. The struggle to build was too much; negative connotations started to fester in my mind.

The same issue 15 years ago is what holds me back, from time to time, today. Yet, my testimony is in the lessons I have learned along the way. We have been taught that faith the size of a mustard seed is beneficial, but the seed needs to be planted in order that it may grow. How deep do you plant it and how will you know? Well, it stems from relationships, specifically, a relationship with the Father in Heaven.

As a business and lifestyle counselor, I teach my clients about building relationships with others in order to sell their products or services. As a business owner, they know how you initially treat people is how those people determine if they purchase from you or not. It also reflects if they will share your business with others.

My relationship with God is no different. I had to develop a deeper relationship with God since becoming an entrepreneur in February 1999. It was necessary because being an entrepreneur, or marketplace minister, if you will, is not about me. It will never be about me, but how God is with me, leads me, and directs my path. My spiritual relationship with my Father in Heaven shows up before I even open my mouth.

In 2013, when I walked away from my marriage and my job, I had to try to reinvent the strong-willed, bold and daring Dana from 1989, coupling her with the new and improved woman of God. I had to get over people and the fear of rejection in order to be the mom, the writer, the coach, and the ministry leader God had called me to be.

Yes, I am a ministry leader; ordained and affirmed as of 2015. This adds to the challenges in all things possible with God for many reasons, not all of them having to do with me being a woman in ministry, that I had to face. Why? Rejection comes in many forms. Without this mustard seed faith, I would have been severely suicidal. I would not be here writing today.

I have gone from homeless to homeowner to renter BACK to homeowner all because of my relationship with the Father and the depth of my faith. I have never gone hungry during any of the challenging times of my life.

Fast forward to 2020, which some have dubbed the year of vision, I have watched God show up for me during a pandemic. I have also looked at all the years I had to sow a seed in order to reap what I have this year. Let me tell you, standing on God's side has been a blessing to my soul, more so than saying I am a Christian.

I have developed another Limited Liability Company for renovation and design, I have obtained certifications necessary for both LLC's, I have worked in the community and helped others see their entrepreneurial potential, and I have grown in the things of God according to His purpose for my life. I put myself on the back burner during the hard times of the pandemic in order to help others get to and from their jobs. God has returned my house to my hands, allowing me to create a process to help other women hold onto their homes, even when it seems all else has failed.

I've learned that faith is deeper than the planting of the mustard seed, because no matter how small I initially start, God is with me to direct and teach me. From those directions and teachings, I grew. It did not happen immediately, and I am glad it did not, or I wouldn't be able to share the truth behind Hebrews 11:1 and my relationship with God.

Dana Williamson

Dana Williamson is a ministry leader for Faith Bureau of Investigations International Ministries, a Business and Lifestyle counselor, as well as speaker, author and publisher. Ms. Williamson has been an entrepreneur for over 20 years, helping women of faith build their businesses continually getting past the fork in the road of their lives. Born and raised in Milwaukee, WI, Dana believes a person of faith can have all that God promised them if they are obedient to the purpose and plan for their lives.

28

Finally Meeting Jesus

▼

by Liz Manz

I haven't always known Jesus. In fact, I only met Him this year. As a child, I had my Bible, and my mother read the stories to me until I could read them myself. My family only went to church on Easter and Christmas. There was no discussion about who God is or why Jesus died. I said my bedtime prayers, but those became fewer and farther in between as I grew older.

My mother always wanted to live in America. She met my father, an American in the Air Force stationed in the United

Kingdom, in 1960. They married not long after and it seemed her American dream was about to come true. Not planned, and according to my mother not wanted, I was born on May 1, 1962, at Milden Hall AFB hospital in England. Mom said that when she saw me for the first time, she realized how much she loved me, and I became the center of her life.

When I turned 8, my mother announced that we were moving to America. That day in June 1970 was perhaps the saddest of my life. Things would be different, but I would adapt. Too sensitive to endure the teasing over my pronunciation of "banana" and "tomato," I quickly rid myself of my English accent. Children of that age don't appreciate being different. By the time I was 10, my mother drank regularly and heavily. I didn't turn to God for help during those years. I thought He didn't care. I was also too ashamed to ask.

I drank, used drugs, hung out with the wrong people, and allowed myself to be used and abused, in an attempt at acceptance. At 18, I left home, if you could call it that. I had moved 14 times in 10 years. My then boyfriend, who later became my husband and the father of my 3 sons, moved to Grass Valley, California. It was there, at 19, that I discovered a fierce maternal instinct that redefined who I was and the future me.

When my youngest was 2, I watched a movie on television about a nuclear bomb exploding in the United States. The focus was on a family who survived the initial event, but whose children would later die from the resulting nuclear fallout. Terrified, with tears in my eyes, I cradled my sleeping babies, and cried out to God, "Please God, protect my babies!" The following day, 2 Jehovah's Witnesses came to my door. I began to study the Bible with them weekly. My husband became violently opposed to this, which made me stop. In secret, I told my sons about God, making sure to silence any discussion on the subject when their father entered the room.

The years passed, my sons grew, and I stopped praying to God to make me a better wife and my husband a better man. After 31 years together, we divorced. The next 8 years I spent alone, not dating nor seeking a relationship. Then one day, I no longer wanted to be alone. I wanted a Christian man with the goal of marriage, but those I met fell far short. About to give up, I saw a profile online, "humble and kind" he said. I met Wesley in November 2019, and the Holy Spirit moved us in unison to begin a Christian life together.

Even after beginning what I felt was a Christian marriage with Wesley, I had not really met Jesus yet. We met for the first time while I was getting ready for work, listening to a book by Max Lucado in my bathroom. Max was describing Jesus's death on the cross in great detail. Hanging on the cross, in agony, pierced and bleeding, His life ebbing away for us, for me. I stood naked, unable to breath, and sobbing uncontrollably. It was in that moment that I met Him, I knew Him, and I loved Him. I knew that He loved me, too. I was baptized in March 2020. Wesley and I were married in August. God is great. Jesus is my Savior. Amen.

Liz Manz

The child of an English mother who married an American stationed in England, Liz remembers moving 14 times in 10 years after coming to America with her parents at the age of 8. As an adult, she was married to the father of her 3 sons for 31 years before they divorced. Liz will always remember 2020 as the remarkable year that Jesus gave her a new life as a born-again Christian and as a wife when she married Wesley, 5 months later.

29

Death to Life

▼

by Pastor Robert Thibodeau

"The mortgage company sent a notice that they are going to start foreclosure proceedings. The electric company put a notice on our door saying in 14 days they will turn off the power. I have no money to buy groceries. What are we going to do?"

Those words from my wife haunted me as I hung up the phone at 11:15 PM on January 25, 1992. I had left my wife and family in Louisiana and traveled to Columbus, GA, to try and sell enough life insurance to take care of my family. Sadly, I had failed yet again.

After leaving the military, I took a position selling life insurance. We made it by my sales, but barely. Then, the first Gulf War started ramping up and my market was deployed. Gone. It's hard to sell insurance when nobody is home.

I decided to go to Columbus, GA (outside of Fort Benning). It was a training center, so they would stay open. That was January 1, 1992. Now, 25 days later, I had sold zero insurance . . . none.

I had failed. I had failed my wife. I had failed my two girls. I was a failure. I went into the little empty bedroom of the dumpy apartment I was renting. It had no furniture. No television. No radio. No bed. I slept on the carpet with a blanket to cover myself.

I started bawling uncontrollably. I hadn't cried like this in years. It seemed like it went on forever. Deep, convulsive cries of despair. "What was I going to do? My family needed money. What can I do?"

A thought just popped into my mind… "You could kill yourself. Your insurance policy is paid up. You've had it three years. Suicide is covered after 2 years. They could pay off all the bills, set aside some money for the girls' college and your wife could live off the rest. They will know you did it for them."

"Yes," I answered, "That's what I'll do." However, I wanted to say good-bye to my wife and kids. They were in bed. I'd have to call them in the morning as they got ready for school.

"Yeah," I thought. "That's what I'll do."

As I laid down on the floor to go to sleep. I noticed the streetlight shining through the venetian blinds and saw it il-luminated my grandfather's Bible. My wife had insisted I take it with me to Georgia and was encouraging me to read it. It was one of the only possessions I had from my grandfa-ther.

My wife was born again in 1983 and had been praying for me to be born again all this time. As I lay there, I thought, "Why not? Tomorrow, at least I'll be able to tell God I read the Bible." In the front of the Bible was a reading list to read the Bible through in one year. I looked up January 25th and it said, "Psalm 34."

I started reading and got down to Verse 7 which said, "The Lord has heard this poor man cry and shall deliver him from all his troubles..."

Immediately, I sensed the room getting brighter and brighter. I closed my eyes and started simultaneously sobbing and laughing uncontrollably! My eyes were closed, but I could sense the presence of Jesus as I cried out through the tears and laughter, "Come into my heart Lord Jesus!"

Then I realized what had happened! God had answered my prayer! I was going to end my life! I was at the "end of myself," and Jesus had now come to GIVE ME A NEW LIFE! I started crying, laughing, and shouting again!

Then, I said to myself, "I have to call my wife." I called and told her what had happened. We both cried and rejoiced. Afterward, I said, "I'm coming home. I can be just as broke with you and the girls at home as I can here. I'm coming home on January 31st."

In the next 5 days, I sold enough insurance to pay the expenses in Georgia and catch up the past due notices with enough left over to buy groceries. My life since then has been transformed. It hasn't always been easy, but God has seen us through the troubling times and has never failed us.

I know for a fact, on January 25, 1992, at 11:35 PM, in a little dumpy apartment in Columbus, Georgia, I WAS BORN AGAIN!

You can know Him, too!

Pastor Robert Thibodeau

Pastor Robert Thibodeau is a 12-year Army veteran, serving as both enlisted and a commissioned Cavalry Officer. He is a retired law enforcement supervisor. After his retirement, he started his radio career. Within 6 months he accepted an opportunity to be on AM radio, nationwide. He is the founder of Podcasters for Christ and helps Christian podcasters, ministers, authors, and musicians, to share the Word through online media, including radio. Please visit https://podcasters forchrist.com for more information.

30

I Didn't Know
It Would Be So Good

▼

by Tom Donnan

May 7, 1983 at 6:30 PM, I invited Jesus into my heart and life. I tell people it was as if I had lived in a dark cave for all of my life. In that instant, Jesus came into my world carrying a light. For the first time I could see. Everything changed. I had lived most of my life trying to forget the first 17 years. From a shy person to a speaker in churches, God is due the glory for how He changed me.

In my Christian walk, it is as if I was born a Pentecostal, but it took experiencing 3 denominations over 30 years for me to discover it. Pastor after pastor didn't know what to think or do with a man who was having God dreams, visions, manifestations, and visitations. It took me 10 years before I found a person to help me know that I was experiencing God.

January 20, 2006 was the beginning of a huge spiritual change for me. During the night, I believe God brought me somewhere to reveal to me that He has a gift He wants to give the Church. It is a gift of His inheritance. Here is the humor of God, on February 6, 2006, just 3 weeks later, I died of what's been nicknamed 'the widow maker' heart attack. I was on my way to the hospital when the vein closed, and I immediately died.

I believe that I went instantly into the afterlife. I was above the ambulance looking at the golf course noticing how peaceful it is and that I am not in pain. Then, the voice of God spoke. It was a deep, masculine sounding voice. His words rolled like thunder. He said one sentence to me, "It is only while you are on earth that you can work for Jesus." When the paramedics hit me with the paddles, I was back in my body. There is nothing more motivating than looking into the face of your own mortality. From that moment on, I have loved working for Jesus.

During my recovery, I thought about how to share this plan God had revealed to me. I believe that the scope of this inheritance that He wants to give is for the majority of the United States known as the Heartland. It begins in Texas and is released in other directions. This brought me to google: "Revival in Texas." Pastor Phillip Corbett's name came up in the number one spot. From that first email, we have become friends. We are now co-authoring, and we minister together. We go to small churches that open their doors to us and pray for the release of God's Holy Spirit. I have seen hundreds of people instantly healed, others delivered, and strongholds broken. Our ministry together continues to this day.

That's God for you! While I was born with a natural mechanical ability, before I was born-again (John 3:7) I was not able to construct a sentence. For me to be an author of 5 books is a testimony to God's provisions. In a dream, God showed me that I needed a publicist. This opened the doors for this once shy person to now be on live television, radio interviews, and all types of other media. There is joy in sharing Jesus with others.

Since 2004, I have been a volunteer for NeedHim.org. It is a partnership between several evangelical organizations to create a safe place for people to talk about what it means to know Jesus Christ. They use media and technology to communicate the Gospel and encourage conversation about what it means to have a personal relationship with Jesus. Anyone with questions can use their phone, chat, text capabilities, or other technology, to reach a live volunteer through NeedHim.org. I have had thousands of conversations sharing Jesus. I tell people about the day that I died, but that I was not a keeper. God threw me back and now I live for Him.

Tom Donnan

Tom Donnan's heart's desire is to share the gospel of Jesus Christ. Life wonderfully changed for him since Jesus came into his life. Now he works to see others blessed by gaining a relationship with Jesus.

Note from our founder, Stephanie Reynolds: It was so exciting to receive Tom's application testimony in the CWC inbox on September 17, 2020. He was and still is on fire for the Lord and he introduced us to NeedHim.org. This ministry is exactly what we needed to connect our readers to a real and caring human being, like Tom, to have an authentic conversation about how a relationship with Jesus changes everything. If you have questions, I encourage you to reach out to Need Him Global, today. Their website is NeedHim.org or you can chat with a volunteer, right now, at https://needhim.org/chat-now/

Closing
Comments

How Jesus Gives You a New Life: God's Plan of Salvation

Congratulations! You've made it to the end of our first book. You've read 30 stories of how Jesus came into each writer's life and turned it around 180 degrees. Perhaps, if you're like me, always short on time or patience, you read the Introduction and maybe three to five testimonies before jumping to these Closing Comments.

Regardless of how you got here, I want to make sure that we have fulfilled our mission to you before you close this book. The mission of each CWC book is to "Encourage, Engage, and Evangelize." I hope everyone who has read this book has been encouraged; believers have chosen to be engaged; and those who didn't know Jesus as their Savior before reading this book, have a personal relationship with Him now. If not, I hope that you start that personal relationship with Jesus by the time you reach the end of these Closing Comments.

On the next few pages are 3 simple steps for beginning your new life in Christ just as all 30 of the CWC members/writers featured in this book have done. Receiving your new life in Christ is as simple as ABC...

A - Accept & Admit

Accept the fact that you've done wrong things and admit that you need forgiveness.

For all have sinned and fall short of the glory of God.
Romans 3:23

For the wages of sin is death. Romans 6:23a

If we confess our sins, he is faithful and just and will forgive us our sins and purify us from all unrighteousness. 1 John 1:9 NIV

B- Believe & Behave

When you believe that Jesus died on the cross and rose bodily from the grave, paying the penalty for your sins, it changes you. That's because when you change what you believe, it changes how you behave.

For God so loved the world that He gave his one and only Son, that whoever believes in Him shall not perish but have eternal life. For God did not send His Son into the world to condemn the world, but to save the world through Him. John 3:16-17

"The time has come," he said. "The kingdom of God has come near. Repent and believe the good news!" Mark 1:15

They replied, "Believe in the Lord Jesus, and you will be saved—you and your household." Acts 16:31

For what I received I passed on to you as of first importance: that Christ died for our sins according to the Scriptures, that He was buried, that he was raised on the third day according to the Scriptures. 1 Corinthians 15:3-4

C- Confess & Choose

Confess Jesus as your Lord and Savior and choose to follow His plan for your life.

> *If you declare with your mouth, "Jesus is Lord," and believe in your heart that God raised Him from the dead, you will be saved. For it is with your heart that you believe and are justified, and it is with your mouth that you profess your faith and are saved.* Romans 10:9-10

> *Then Jesus said to his disciples, "Whoever wants to be My disciple must deny themselves and take up their cross and follow Me.* Matthew 16:24

> *For I am not ashamed of the gospel, because it is the power of God that brings salvation to everyone who believes: first to the Jew, then to the Gentile.* Romans 1:16

> *Everyone who calls on the name of the Lord will be saved.* Romans 10:13

If you've carefully and prayerfully read through these ABCs, but you still have questions, or you don't feel like anything has changed—no worries. The first 'test' of your faith may be to believe that you've been forever changed because the Bible says so, regardless of your feelings.

Another name for the salvation experience is being "born again" (John 3:7). Some people are spiritually born-again with a thirst for God's Word similar to a healthy newborn baby's desire for milk. Other Christian newborns have to cultivate a taste for God's word. Whether you're spiritually born into that first group, the second, or somewhere in between, it's important to develop the habit of reading God's Word daily. Like that baby needs milk to live, to grow, and to remain healthy, a steady diet of God's Word is essential to the healthy spiritual growth of a newborn Christian, too.

There's a long list of other things that a newborn Christian has in common with a newborn baby. While the innocence of newborns makes them so adorable, it makes them incredibly vulnerable, too. The same is true of baby Christians. I'm so grateful to the two older women who counseled me on Sunday, April 10, 1983, the day I asked Jesus to come into my heart and change me. While they rejoiced with me and celebrated the fact that if I had died that very moment, I could rest assured that I'd be on my way to Heaven, they also warned me that my decision to trust Jesus had made me an enemy of satan. My new status as a player on God's team was not to be taken lightly considering how much the devil hates the fact that he will never be equal to God. These wise women warned me that things in my life could get worse before they got better, now that I was saved. It was only a few weeks before I understood exactly about what they had warned me. Thankfully, even a bad day with Jesus is better than my best day as a sinner destined to join satan in Hell.

The summary of the last few paragraphs, the last few pages, and this entire book is, of course, Jesus can give you a new life and when He does, it's just the beginning. Get growing as soon as you're born again. It's one of the few decisions in life that you will never regret.

If you still have some questions about this life-changing decision, I'd suggest going back a few pages to the last testimony in this book, "I Didn't Know It Would Be So Good," by Tom Donnan. Tom introduced me and the CWC to NeedHim.org. We introduce this great organization to you at the end of his testimony. NeedHim.org gives you the opportunity to quickly connect with a volunteer in order to have "an authentic conversation about how a relationship with Jesus changes everything." Volunteers are available 24/7 to help you and "to bring glory to God"—the two best reasons to do anything, if you ask me. —*Stephanie*